Morrissey's
Perfect Pint

Morrissey's Perfect Pint

Neil Morrissey
&
Richard Fox

Collins

Contents

☞ The pub

☞ Food

There'll be plenty of time to drink Kaliber when you die.

Introduction

'For a quart of ale is a dish for a king.'

The Winter's Tale

So Foxy and me are in this pub: the staff really wish we weren't there, the beer tastes like badger poo, the food's been through Abu Ghraib and the music is so loud our teeth are bleeding. I shout at Foxy, 'Mate, it doesn't have to be like this', and the picture of the perfect pub floats into our minds. At this moment the idea is born to set up our own pub *and* brew our own beer in an on-site microbrewery. Bloke Heaven: beer, pub and home become one. 'Fancy a pint?' 'Yep.' 'Love, just nipping downstairs. Be back in an hour …'

We need a different kind of pub now to the pulling joints of youth. Pulling is still on the cards, but in a more genteel way: tugging, let's say. Pubs need to reflect our age and our desire for the three Qs: quality food, quality beer and quality service. This is what *The Perfect Pint* is all about.

The problem is that our generation created the monster of the high street chain bar. It is exactly what we wanted when we were 18 (instead of those sticky carpet horror shows of the 70s and 80s) but the monster has escaped and killed every other kind of boozer in its path. The opportunity for beer drinking, as we now want to do it, is getting squeezed out by these characterless, sterile vomit hovels. At this point in our lives we want something different.

Pubs are closing their doors at the rate of nearly 60 a week. But these 'establishments' where you get crap service, crap beer, crap wine, crap food, crap atmosphere and a crap fight at the end of the night are taking over the high street. Nothing about them has anything to do either with pubs or continental cafés – they're the spawn of corporate marketing departments interested in creating a template for 'customer experience'. Britain's attempt at sophisticated la-di-da café culture has replaced sticky carpets with sticky stripped wooden floors and cardboard food with

cardboard canapés. The pub's evolution seems to have missed out a stage, the stage in which there is a place to drink, in a community, with decent local food and decent local beer. And good service!

The plan, then, was simple: find a pub, buy it, renovate it to the way we want a pub to look, brew our own beer and cook great food. In other words, create the perfect pub serving the perfect pint. Of course, the logistics are staggering, it's costing us an arm and a leg and there are no guarantees that the whole venture won't go tits up. But we believe that people respond to quality, and that's what we're all about. Great beer, great food and a great atmosphere to drink and eat in.

Our first attempt at a brew is described on page 15. While we were waiting for it to ferment, we decided to write down everything we love, hate, know and don't know about beer, pubs, women and life. And drinking. Oh yes, drinking. This is the result – a beer book for blokes. Keep it in the little boys' room.

☞ **Beer**

Drinking
The Pub
Food

*'If God had intended us to drink beer,
He would have given us stomachs.'*

David Daye

Beer in history

Beer, when you get down to it, is about life. The kind of beer you drink (or don't), where you drink it, the mates you drink it with, all define you more than your job or your clothes. Beer has a history and a culture that reaches right around the world and way back in time to Ancient Egypt and then some. It was with us at the dawn of civilisation and will be around until we end up in the gutter of this or another planet.

But what do we know about it?

Morrissey: Beer is the national drink of Britain, about the only thing that will always come in imperial measures (milk, petrol, anyone?) and thank God for that. And thank God for natural yeasts. Fermentation was probably discovered accidentally, when some stored grain got wet, thereby softening the kernel of the grain and allowing yeasts in the air to do their magic.

> **Foxy:** So beer is also, contrary to widespread opinion, the reason we're civilised. The need to store grain to make beer led to settled communities, where the art of brewing was developed, and we could all get down to some serious drinking – excellent!

M: Beer brewing, from barley, was actually well-established in Britain by the time the Romans got here in the first century AD. The Roman Emperor Julian thought beer smelt disgusting compared with wine – like 'goat' compared with 'nectar'. Maximus Toolus we call him.

Anyway, making wine was a no-no in Britain because of the climate which is much better suited to growing grains than grapes.

It is to our eternal chagrin that it was Germans, in the form of colonising Anglo-Saxons, who brought the beer habit with them to England in the fifth century AD. The Germans! I suppose we should be grateful that it wasn't the French. Anyway the Germans called it 'ol' or 'ale' and from about the sixth century beer, from the Latin word 'biber', meaning drink.

> **F:** I knew you had a good education. Right through the Dark and Middle Ages, making beer was quite rightly seen as an essential part of everyday life. It was safer than drinking water because it had been boiled, and provided nutrition in the form of carbohydrates and protein when food was scarce. Brewing was women's work, and 'ale-wives' prepared the beer alongside the bread, until the 16th century, when commercial brewing and the influence of the Church prevailed.

M: People don't realize what a big part the Church played in the development of beer. They brewed beer to refresh pilgrims, and licensed binge drinking among rural folk to help them let off steam safely and raise money. Three-day sessions weren't uncommon! Monasteries brewed untold amounts of ale and monks drank a skinful. The daily allowance for monks at Burton Abbey in the year 1004 was two gallons (16 pints) of ale!

> **F:** That explains why they took brewing to new heights of sophistication – they needed advanced techniques to guarantee copious amounts of quality product. The most significant development was the use of hops which gives beer its 'bitter' taste but, more importantly, preserves it. Dutch traders brought beer to Britain and by the 1520s was here to stay. The basic recipe of beer as we know it was created: barley, yeast, water and hops.

M: Celebration ales were brewed to mark everything! 'Bride-ales' or 'bridals' (or 'bridles' if the wife-to-be was a bit of a horse) were made to celebrate weddings. They were brewed by the Lucky Lady herself, and sold to raise a dowry for the couple for whom, in those days, 'life meant life'. Eye-weepingly strong 'groaning-ales' were fermented, often for seven or eight months, to help mothers-to-be through the painful birthing process – and the expectant fathers, of course. The baby was then often washed in the beer because …

> **F:** …it was safer than water! Recycled grain was used to make 'small beer', which was the piss-weak everyday stuff given to women and children and served at breakfast. The better stuff was given to farm-workers, prescribed by doctors, used in religious ceremonies and other celebrations. You didn't need to have a drink problem to have a drink problem in those days.

M: Which isn't to deny that getting muntered was high on everybody's agenda. Because there was no way to measure or control the alcoholic content, apart from re-brewing the grains to make 'small beer', ale was often wickedly strong. The eighth-century missionary, St Boniface, wrote that in Britain 'the vice of drunkenness is too frequent. This is an evil peculiar to pagans and to our race. Neither the Franks nor the Gauls nor the Lombards nor the Romans nor the Greeks commit it.'

> **F:** Interestingly, drinking from glasses didn't occur until much later. People drank out of pigskin pitchers, horns and bowls which couldn't be put down like a glass, so 'down in one' was common. Communal bowls were marked by pegs and pins, indicating where one customer's portion of ale started and finished. Drinking more than your fair share became known as 'taking someone down a peg or two'. One novelty of the late 17th century was the whistling tankard, which had a whistle at the bottom so you could call the landlord when you needed a top up!

M: That's one for the *Innovations* catalogue, methinks. Another change in the 17th century was a bit of a disaster. Because they were worried about losing revenue, the King and Parliament cut duties on gin to encourage people to drink it instead of French brandy. Imagine their surprise when this produced an epidemic of gin-necking which made today's so-called binge drinking look like a tea dance in Rhyl.

F: And gin in those days was the original rocket fuel, often over double the strength of today's sophisticated aperitif. This had the unintended but gratifying effect of making beer drinking respectable by comparison. William Hogarth, the 18th century artist, made two engravings called *Beer Street* and *Gin Lane* that showed the former as an ordered, happy, pleasant environment and the latter as a horror-filled chaos.

M: Like Harrogate on a Saturday night but actually much worse. The 18th century saw the big commercial brewers establish themselves and take most of the business from small, independent brewers who had been the backbone of British beer-making. Science helped with devices like the steam engine and hydrometer which allowed larger quantities to be brewed with greater precision. Also, better roads meant cheaper, mass-produced beer could be transported to places that had previously relied on alewives and alcoholic monks for their bevvy.

F: Ah yes, science. In the 19th century Louis Pasteur dealt the small beer producers a double whammy when he grew yeast in the laboratory, meaning that brewers no longer had to rely on wild, airborne yeasts for fermentation. He also invented 'pasteurisation', which meant beer could be easily treated to stay fresh longer. Beer remained a mainstay of the working man's diet until well into the 20th century when food became more plentiful. Industrialisation also saw a drop in the demand for physical labour, which meant more machines powered by oil and less men fuelled by beer. The world changed, Neil.

M: Indeed it did, Foxy. The invasion of bland German lagers, in the 60s, when TV advertising emerged and teenagers flexed their drinking muscles at the pub, saw a big decline in beer drinking, but there are signs of a comeback, with the growth of artisan breweries and specialist beers. It may not be the lifeblood of the nation, as it was in pre-industrial times, but it is still a vital part of life and undoubtedly our national drink. Cheers!

Our first brew

So, how do you make it? Do you want to try? Honestly, you would not believe how easy it is to come up with a good brew. Seven days, a bit of kit, and a lot of patience is all you need. Look in the directory at the back of this book for a list of top suppliers. The stuff you can get these days is way ahead of the pot noodle in a bucket they sold back in the 70s. Here's what you need.

Brewing beer is as easy as cooking pasta. If you can boil a kettle and follow a recipe, you can make your own home-brew. The ingredients you need are:

1 **Malt** Malt is mostly made of barley. The barley will give the whole tone of the beer; it's the canvas on which you paint your flavours. The colour of the beer is strongly linked to the malt from which it is made.
2 **Hops** Each type of hop adds a different level and variety of bitterness. Using more than one variety or type of hops add to the depth of flavour of the beer.
3 **Yeast** This is the ingredient that transforms the sugar in the wort (the liquid) into alcohol, so treat it with respect.
4 **Liquor** Traditional brewers call water 'liquor'. And good liquor makes good beer. The most prized water contains happy balances of minerals, particularly calcium, and plays a vital part in brewing beer. At one time, Burton-upon-Trent was home to more than 200 breweries largely because the water supply made it ideal for the production of English ales. Breweries today can adjust almost any water supply to produce just the right balance of minerals.

You'll also need some basic equipment: 25-litre plastic bucket with lid (the mash tun); bottles and caps; hydrometer (for checking sugars and alcohol strength); thermometer; measuring jugs which can hold more than 20 litres; siphoning tube; fermentation bucket; sanitisers.

Here's our first brew recipe. And guess what, we thought it was fucking marvellous.

Morrissey and Foxy's Blonde Ale

MAKES ABOUT 40 PINTS

Ingredients:

4,080g	Golden Promise malt
260g	Light crystal malt
39g	Styrian Golding hops
32g	Fuggles hops
10g	Irish moss
15g	Cascade hops
1	packet fast acting yeast

Method:

Add 23 litres of water heated to 77°C to the mash tun. Allow the temperature to drop to 72°C and add both malts. Stir to form a thick porridge. Maintain temperature between 62°C and 69°C for 1½ hours. Strain wort (the liquid) into a large pan very slowly. If the liquid is not clear, return to the mash tun and repeat until a clear wort is produced. Using a watering can, spray the leftover malt with water heated to 77°C. Continue to do this until a reading of 1005 is reached on the hydrometer. Top up the boiler to the desired level and heat to a rolling boil. Add the Styrian Golding and Fuggles hops and the Irish Moss. Boil vigorously for 1 hour. Add the Cascade hops and boil for a further 15 minutes. Cool very quickly and transfer the liquid only to the fermenting vessel. Add the dissolved yeast, cover and place in a cool (22°C degree) room for two days. Carefully siphon off the clear liquid into another fermenting vessel, leaving behind any flotsam and jetsam. Ferment for a further three or four days with an airtight lid. Siphon off the clear BEER and enjoy!

Top tips for a special brew

Like everything in life, there are rules and shortcuts that can make it all so much easier. Here come Morrissey and Foxy's Top Tips for brilliant brewing.

1. Use High-Quality, Fresh Ingredients.
Like everything else, you get what you pay for. Fresh ingredients make better home-brew. Simple. If you started with dry yeast, move up to liquid yeast. Store the ingredients properly. Most will go off over time so use them up quickly. You know what that means? More Beer!

2. Do your Homework.
Making a decent home-brew is a craft, and the more experienced you become, the better the beer. Browse the internet for advice on techniques, find a local artisan brewer (there will be one) and pester them until they take out a restraining order. Whether their beer is good, bad or ugly, they'll know some mistakes to avoid, and possibly have gems of advice to scatter your way. Check out some of the top beer books which are easy to find these days. Basically turn into a beer bore.

3. Keep it Clean.
Proper cleaning is essential if you want to make really good beer. Anything that is going to come into contact with your beer needs to be spotless, so keep your kit sterilised. If you don't, bacteria and other infections will get a grip and spoil your brew. Don't end up with a pint of 'Olde Thrushe'. The period just before fermentation is when beer is at its most vulnerable. See the *Directory* page 145 for specialist cleaners.

4. Cool the Wort Quickly.

Cooling your wort quickly will reduce the chance of bacterial infection –
placing its container in a sink filled with cold water and ice cubes will do
the job. Though contamination isn't harmful, it can make the beer taste
and smell like road kill.

5. Amounts and temperatures.

In addition to doing your homework, there'll be a certain amount of trial
and error with ingredients and processes. To start with, try to follow the
recipe guidelines closely. At least you can blame someone else if it doesn't
work. After a few batches, however, you'll find out what works best and
what's total bollocks.

6. Buy long-term Kit.

If you are new to brewing, you'll probably buy an off-the-shelf kit to get
started. Nothing wrong with that. If you like brewing (and you will), make
the next stage up count. Get some decent kit that will last you in the long-
term, rather than something you're going to have to trade up from next
year. Speak to the experts (see page 145) or your brewing Yoda. They'll
point you in the right direction.

Beer glossary

Adjuncts Beer-making term for starch other than from malted barley or wheat, such as corn starch, rice or sugar. A source of fermentable sugars in cheaper beers.

Barrel A unit of measurement. In Britain, a barrel holds 36 gallons. In the USA, a barrel holds 31.5 US gallons (considerably less).

Brew Kettle Vessel used in the brewing process, to heat the wort.

Bright Tasting term used to describe a beer's brilliance and clarity.

Filtration Beer is normally filtered to remove dead yeast cells and other insoluble particles to achieve a brilliantly clear finished beer. Many ales are 'live' and unfiltered.

Finish Beer-tasting term describing how long the flavour of a beer lingers on the palate after swallowing. Longer is generally better.

Grain One of the four ingredients of beer along with water, yeast and hops. Grain is a generic term for barley, wheat and other cereal crops used in beer making.

Grist Beer-making term for the milled grain to be used in fermentation.

Hogshead Traditional unit of measurement: a cask holding 54 gallons.

Lauter Tun A piece of brewing equipment, the tun filters the mostly liquid wort from the solid mash.

Liquor: The quality of the water that is used to brew is an important factor in the flavour of the beer. Brewers refer to the water they work with as 'liquor'.

Mash The mash is the mixture of malt and water.

Pasteurisation Heating of beer to 60-79°C to stabilise it microbiologically.

Pils (Pilsener) Style of bottom-fermented light-coloured beer with a very pronounced taste of hops.

Porter A very dark, top-fermented beer first brewed in London in the 18th century.

Sparge To spray grist with hot water to remove soluble sugars (maltose). This takes place at the end of the mash.

Trappist Ale Produced in Belgium by just six registered monastic breweries, who together make up membership of the 'International Trappist Association'. Trappist ales are characterised by the use of special yeast strains and sugars in their production.

Wort The liquid extract that is created from the mash. This sugary liquid is then fermented into beer. (Pronunciation is key with this one – a very heavy roll on the 'r' is required.)

Zymurgy The science of beer brewing.

'I'll have a pint of ...'

Once you've sparged your wort (trickled water through it to extract the sugars), drained your mash tun and let your yeast go wild, you can bottle your beautiful brew up and look forward to hours of lovely drinking. But don't forget that, while supping away, you need to give the liquid a name. We're not talking about 'Tis Our Own' or anything crap like that. For beer you need earthy, bestial names to make your fellow drinkers proud of the beer's heritage.

Dog Bolter · Happy New Beer · **Rudolph's Revenge**
Seriously Bad Elf · **Daggy Sheep** · Old Legover
Bishop's Finger · Dizzy Dick · **Another Fine Mess**
Buddy Confusing · **Dark Vader** · Old Pants Down
Cojones · Big Black Handful · **Old Pig's Bottom**
Daggy Pig · **Sticky Tacky Tackle** · Piddle in the Sun
Milk the Stout Nipple · Research · **Bugger Me**
This · That · **Pokey Old Hole** · Dead Badger
Olde Speckled Wart · **Olde Dribbly Bottom**
Stick-on Beard · **Olde Twig** · Big Milky Gibbet
Arsehole · Kneehammer · **Office Party**
Olde Flibbertigibbet · The Usual

Some non-alcoholic beer names

If you're teetotal, well, first of all, fair play to you for getting this book; second, you're allowed to call – gulp – non-alcoholic beers imaginative names too. Here are some of the ones we came up with.

Why? · Get A Life · **Limp** · Olde Dull Maid
Sensible · PG · **Old Zzzzzzzz**

Types of beer

How was it for you? We took our first brew out onto the streets of Yorkshire to check and it went down a storm. One thing you learn pretty quickly is how different each brew can turn out – especially if you're making small quantities at home. You also learn the vast range of beer types you can choose from. Check out our list of home-brew suppliers in the directory at the back.

Beer is a brown drink with a foamy head, or a piss-coloured, fizzy drink called lager, right? Wrong. There are as many types of beer as there are types of women – more even. Here's our guide to some of the tastiest, foxiest and downright psycho …

Belgian 'wild' beers

Really *crazy* beers, with fermentation being left to 'wild' yeasts in the air – just like in days of yore. Whereas modern breweries are cleaner than a nun's panties, these Belgian 'Lambic' brewers go more for the British hospital approach to hygiene. Windows are left open, moulds encouraged to fester – anything to get those free-thinking yeasts in to have their way with the brew.

The beer equivalent of an orgy – takes place spontaneously, with random partners; you never quite know what the outcome will be.

Wheat beers

Also often called 'white' to confuse things. This fresh and feisty style is another Belgian classic, a great thirst quencher – better than cheap, lager piss by a country mile. Often cloudy (hence 'white'), the husk of wheat make it a tricky little customer for the brewer and it often clogs the brewing vessels.

Foxy little blonde – easy, a bit thick, but fresh as you like and liable to leave you wanting more on a hot summer's day.

Porters and stouts

Dark, heavy beers that get their burnt fruit flavour from the roasting of malts at high temperatures. Thick, gooey beers – think *Guinness*, think *Beamish* with knobs on. Sadly porters are not much around today, though obviously popular in Ireland – and Alaska for some reason.
Strong, dark, body and creamy head is an acquired taste not easily forgotten!

Celtic beers

At this point a word or two about our Celtic friends in Ireland and Scotland is probably in order. Without wanting to give a history lesson, it's worth noting a few differences in brewing, which have left a beer legacy in these fine countries today.

It was a Celtic tradition to use bittering herbs like heather, cereals and fruits to flavour the beer, because hops were difficult to grow, and expensive to import from southern England. Even if you could overcome the shame of it. Small breweries have revived this practice and their beers are proving very popular with the punters and beer writers alike. Pine cones and seaweed are among the ingredients being used to give a unique Caledonian tang to today's beers. And not just because they're free.

Shilling

One of the things an English beer drinker will notice when entering the land of kilts and free prescriptions is how much the Scots go on about England and the English.

Another thing is the need for a whole new vocabulary at the pump – the language of shillings. No, this is not a cheap joke about wallets and cobwebs. At your average Scottish bar, you'll have the choice of a pint of 60/– or 70/–. Perhaps an 80/– or 90/– if you're feeling adventurous.

These shilling ('/–') categories reflect the prices charged for a barrel of beer in the 19th century. The stronger the beer, the more it cost, hence 60/-, 70/-, 80/- and 90/–. Just to make things easy, these categories were also known as 'light', 'heavy', 'export' and 'wee heavy', with 'wee heavy' being the strongest, as well as the easiest to make a joke from.

The shilling names fell out of favour but were revived in the 70s, and we think they're great. McCheers!

Can be heavy-going, but will keep you warm in winter.

Dark Irish beers

In Ireland, *Guinness* is a national icon, up there with James Joyce and Roy Keane. Yet a lot of people don't know that the origins of the big G are in a dark beer popular with the porters at Covent Garden market in London. When this was exported to Dublin, Arthur Guinness decided to take on the challenge, and he did like a challenge. In the early days BG (Before *Guinness*), when Dublin authorities threatened to cut off his water supply, he threatened to pickaxe the gang who came to dry him out. You didn't mess with Arthur.

Anyway, so successful was he at brewing 'porter', or Dublin Stout as it became known in Ireland, that he switched his entire beer production to it in 1799, and the rest is definitely history.

It's not all *Guinness* though, oh no. There's another strand of brewing in Ireland that has been making a bit of a comeback recently and that's Irish ales, or Irish red ales. These get their name from the reddish hue produced by roasting small quantities of barley in the brewing process – it's very popular with beer connoisseurs.

Definitely good for you, with a strong body and frothy top!

American artisan beers

We Brits took beer with us when we colonised America. Then immigrants from Germany brought their lager styles to the Yanks. Now the trad Brit styles are making a comeback in the States, with artisan brewers – from the West Coast to the East – producing everything from strong, so-called 'barley wines' to savoury brown ales (like our *Newcastle Brown*).

A marriage made in heaven – strong British roots and American savvy.
Pull one of these and you won't regret it.

German beers

Though they do produce their own 'sour' beers, the Germans are rightly best known for inventing the lager – named after the lagering ('bedding') method of bottom-fermenting beer (as opposed to ale, which is generally top-fermenting beer)! There are loads of different types of lager made all over the world, not just the cheap piss beloved of British city-centre pubs. It is one hell of a drink when done properly ('hell' meaning 'light-coloured' or 'fair' being the German word of choice to describe the golden brew).

Ice-cool blonde. May appear common, but worth bedding for a while to fully appreciate.

Fruit beers

Nothing to do with the cherry-on-a-stick brigade. Beers have been flavoured with fruit for centuries – raspberry, apricot, cherry and peach are favourites and are popular with those wildly experimental Belgian Lambic brewers and also American microbrewers. The fruit balances the acidity and acts as a thirst quencher. More disturbingly, some brewers use vegetables like pumpkin and chilli to give their brews a kick. Now that's just confusing.

Colourful, though may be just a little tart.

MORRISSEY MAXIM

A great pub is like your best mate – familiar, comforting and a bit smelly.

Spit or swallow: Morrissey and Foxy's guide to beer tasting

Why taste beer?

If you think brewing your own is a step too far towards wearing hairy jumpers and having a twiggy beard, why not get a load of different beers in and have a tasting session with some mates? (Do this at home, not at the pub – you'll look like a complete twat.) The point of brewing your own is that you are in control of the taste. By finding out what flavours and styles of beer appeal, you open your mind and mouth to some of the 5,000 or so different brands of beer you can get in the UK at the moment. So when people say 'I don't drink beer, only lager', we say, 'Yes, you do drink beer – lager's a beer. You're halfway there. Now, come on, take a look along that bar, past the chemical piss. See those pumps? Go on!'

When you were a teenager you didn't say, 'No long trousers for me, I'll stick with the shorts, thanks.' We change – tastes change. It's in the interest of some hefty marketing budgets that we Keep Drinking The Same Thing, but we don't have to do as we're told. There's a whole world of beer out there, just waiting to be discovered. Some of it you'll hate, some you wouldn't bother with again, but one or two you might like. Then love. Then search for more. Why deny yourself the pleasure? You may have been drinking the same pint for 20 years, but it's never too late to try other things. A lot of this is about drinking for flavour as opposed to drinking because it's coloured blue and it gets you off your tits when you've had seven of them. Get drunk on something decent. Let's have fun, but quality fun.

The tasting session

When you taste something you are excited by, ask yourself, 'Why? What's the thing in that beer that makes my trousers tingle?' When someone buys you a beer and you don't like it, do the same thing – what is it about that beer that makes you think of snogging your granny?

So, get the beers you want to try and read the labels to find out what's the best temperature to drink them at. The cooler the beer, though, the less flavour and smell it gives off. There's a reason that some lager is supercold: it tastes like Chernobyl water at anything other than lip-freezing temperatures.

1. **Pour into a wine glass.** Have a look at the colour of the beer by holding it against a sheet of white paper or a white cloth. Most beer (except wheat beers) should be clear. If not, something may have gone wrong at the processing stages and some rubbish has slipped in. Chuck the beer down the khazi if that's the case.

2. **Swirl.** Hold the glass by the stem and examine the colour for shade and intensity.

3. **Smell.** You'll get some initial smells, which you should shout out very quickly – all of the impressions you get are valid. Remember what gives trouser action from the smell. Try different words until you nail the smell. There are some ideas in the Flavour Wheel (page 29) but have a go at saying what comes into your head first of all.

4. **Taste.** Finally, get some beer into your mouth. Swill the glass and take a sip; get some air in your mouth at the same time as this will help get more flavours out. Try not to breathe in too hard or you'll choke – just a tip. Swirl the beer round so all of your mouth gets a taste. Make ridiculous noises, puff your cheeks out – do anything that helps move the beer around and gets it going. The more you do, the more tastes you'll get. Keep a mental note of what you get – don't shout out as your mates won't be happy with a faceful of gobby beer. When you swallow, try to breathe out through your nose. This will increase the flavour extraction. If beer comes out of your nose, you've done it wrong. 'Dead

badger on the motorway' or 'twig in autumn leaves and fox do', perhaps gentle 'rose petals with a hint of *Glade* fruits of the forest'? Whatever works for you …

Beer tasting words

If you're really serious you can write down your reactions. Here's a list of things 'professional' beer tasters (bugger of a job) write down when they taste a brew.

Appearance Things to note are colour, how long the head lasts for, presence or absence of 'floaties' …

Smell Someone who knows about this stuff said that your perception of it is dulled after about four sniffs – so make the most of each one. It can be broken down into three entirely separate parts: aroma, bouquet and odour.

Aroma comes from the malt, grain, and anything produced by the fermentation. Aromas that come from the malt and grain are often described as nutty, sweet, grainy and malty. The fresh, earthy quality of malted barley combined with the bitter, apparently antiseptic aroma of hops gives the beer its aroma. Is there a strong hop or a faint hop smell? Is there a malt character? Is it full or light?

Bouquet comes entirely from the hops. Stick your nose in the glass straight after pouring to discover the bouquet as it evaporates quickly. Different hop varieties contribute different qualities to the bouquet, and some may not be appropriate for some styles. Terms used to describe the hop aroma include herbal, pine, floral, resin and spice.

Odour is only remarked on (in beer-tasting circles, don't you know) if there's something wrong. It's the equivalent of the 'floaty' when you look at the beer, or a fart in a lift. Skunkiness is apparently a favourite word here. Other words are butter, sulphury, cooked vegetable, fishy, oily and chlorine.

Taste This is the moment we're all here for. There are three stages to taste – front, middle and finish. This has nothing to do with where you taste different things on your tongue but the taste as you drink – from sip to swallow. One good tip is only to swallow as much as will cover your tongue – that way all parts (and taste categories – sweet, sour, salty, bitter and umami – (the Japanese word for savoury) are noticeable.

Other questions the pros ask include: Is the hop taste and the malt taste in the right mixture? Is the body full or thin? What happens after you've swallowed – does the taste stick around for a while? This is called the length … a good beer, like so many things, will have length …

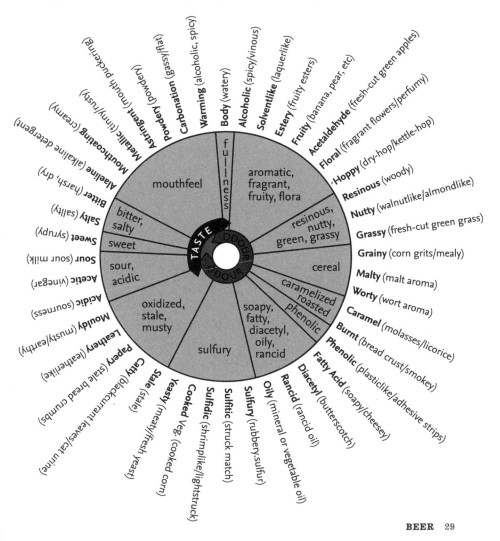

Twelve other uses for beer

When the lady of the house says she can't get her salad in the fridge because of all the beers, use this guide to convince her that a Beer's Not Just For Drinking – It's For Life. Of course it's mostly bollocks, but then again ...

1. Beer bath
Sounds too good to be true? The latest craze in some European spas is sitting in a tub of beer for half an hour. Beer contains a vitamin B complex that is great for the skin, apparently. And the hops in beer relax the body.

2. Washing hair
Are you having trouble with your runaway barnet? Washing your hair with beer will make it softer and give it more body. Every bloke's dream when you think about it. 'What's that smell?' 'Oh, I've been washing my hair.' Even works for slapheads, but remember to keep your mouth open.

3. Fire extinguisher
OK – not a REAL one. And definitely not electrical fires – shocking. But give it a shake and it will put out small fires. Like from the grill. 'Which is why we should keep some in the fridge *at all times*, darling.'

4. Lawn care
Get rid of those brown spots – spray them with beer! The fermented sugars in ale kill fungi. So when you spill a can while sitting in the garden you're 'conditioning the lawn'.

5. Loosen rusty bolts
'Why are you out here in the garage drinking again?' 'Drinking? I'm applying beer to these bike parts, because the carbonation will get rid of the rust. When that's done I'll cycle to the offie for more of this wonder cure!'

6. Stop snoring
Simply put a can in a sock and attach it to the back of a T-shirt with a safety pin. Put on before staggering to bed. The can will stop you sleeping on your

back, which will reduce your nocturnal emissions. Well some of them. And use a can, not a bottle. No, I'm not nagging you. Well, if you'd only listen.

7. Mouse killer
It's best to use 'Value Lager' for this. Fill a bucket about a third of the way up and lean a piece of wood against the side, so the mice can climb to the top, sniff the beer and jump in. Still a spectator sport in some parts of Eastern Europe, we're told.

8. Getting rid of a kidney stone
Nasty little buggers, kidney stones. Still, if you've got one, beer can open up the tubes connecting the kidneys and bladder, making it easier to pass. Cranberry juice works well too, but have you *tasted* it? Also alcohol numbs the pain. Doesn't it just?

9. Calming a (mild) stomach-ache
This is great. The carbonated beer will help settle your stomach and the alcohol content reduces any pain. Beer – the cure to all our problems!

10. Scale fish
Attach four bottle tops to a piece of wood so the lips are facing out. Scrape the fish, but away from you if you don't want to end up looking like Jeff Goldblum in *The Fly*.

11. Marinate meat
Next time your Better Half is soaking some meat in dry white wine, soak yours in some gutsy beer. They both tenderise the meat, but we know which one will taste better.

12. Polishing furniture
Rub your wooden furniture with a cloth soaked in flat beer. It will polish it and make it look like new. Another good one if caught armed with ale in the garden at 'Beer Zero' time (*Drinktionary,* page 72).

Beer and your body

Let's face it, the primary purpose of beer is to induce pleasures of many kinds. But let's not forget that these pleasures bring perils to the poor human body. Everything has a cost (even if you're only 20 and haven't found that out yet – look at your dad). Remember, moderation in all things is wise and, if you can't quite manage it, then these are some of the consequences. Let's take a scientific look at:

Farting – beer does unblock the old wind tunnel. When they introduced the smoking ban in Scotland, certain things became apparent that had long been hidden. One man was barred from a pub because of his stinky bottom burps. It turns out that he'd been sitting in the same pub for over ten years, night after night, producing noxious odours, but no one had noticed because of the smell of smoke. On his way out of the pub, some of the following phrases may have been shouted after him – all of them in the best possible taste.

Cut the cheese · Crack a rat · **Step on a duck**
Stink burger · **Ass blaster** · Toilet tune
Silent but deadly · Poop gas · **Steamer** · Rip one
Let one fly · **Uncorked symphony** · Let one go
Backdoor breeze · Pop a fluffy · **Kill the canary**
Gas attack · **Jockey burner** · Cut loose · **Nose death**
Backfire · Stink bomb · **Gas blaster** · Odorama
Bun shaker · Tail wind · **Sphincter song**
Lethal cloud · **Crowd splitter** · Bean blower
Moon gas · What the dog did · **Burnin' rubber**
Anal volcano · **Foul howl** · Fog slicer · **Odour
bubble** · **Air bagel** · Roast the jockeys
Squeak one out · Gas master · **Spit a brick** · Lay a
wind loaf **The toothless one speaks**

Tackle issues – we all think we're God's Gift after a certain point in the evening (see *The beer drinker's guide to romance and seduction* page 57) ,but, let's face it, the beer can do bad things to your ladies' friend. If you break the ten-pint barrier, you may find yourself:

Singing with Flacido Domingo
Sticking spaghetti in the parking meter
Giving coin to the fuck beggar
In the county of Wiltshire
Limping with intent
Taking the gold at the flaccid Olympics
Lighting a damp firework
Trying to wake Sleeping Beauty without a kiss
Starring in Deadwood
In the cold meats' section
With Ascension Deficit Disorder
Welcomed to Flaccid City. Population: You
Trying to fill a cone with Mister Softee
Turning off the lights before the party
At Viagra Falls
Getting fanny fright
In possession of a Vegan erection
Graduating from Limp Dick University with honours
With soggy cashew nut syndrome

Gentlemen's toilet – there's a rule that has to be observed early on in a sesh: take as long as possible before you 'break the seal'. As soon as you go once, you'll not stop all night. Best to cross your legs and hang on to your water, then you'll have more beer time.

Skin – if you drink a lot of beer your body dehydrates, which is great for giving you that rugged, craggy, sunburnt look that is apparently such a hit with the ladies …

Brain – turns to mush. You think you're a suave, seductive genius while actually you're shouting loudly about pants and dribbling from the side of your mouth. In the morning, your brain will be twice its natural size and screaming to get out of your skull – welcome to Hangover Land; just turn right after The Top Shelf (see *Drinktionary*, page 72).

Legs – aside from the immediate 'legs made of overcooked pasta' display as you leave the pub, long-term heavy drinking can give you GOUT. If you thought that was a disease that, like smallpox, was killed off so many centuries ago, think again. Gout is alive and well and living in the big toe of the resident bar-propper at your local.

Hands – if you think the global economy is shaky, try lighting a match after a week-long bender.

Beach physique – as you hit a certain point in your life, no matter how often you get off the bus a stop early, the inches keep creeping on to your waistline. Your once-perfect physique (maintained regardless of how many chip butties and pints you threw down your neck) is starting to bulge. Welcome to middle-aged spread. Pints of beer help it along nicely; if you get very good at it, your stomach can get big enough (and near enough) to rest your pint on without danger of spillage.

MORRISSEY MAXIM

Treat your woman like your beer – pump her gently but firmly until she's got a good head on her.

Your good health, sir

We all know that beer is good for you but we would never claim any of the following. These may not stand up in court, but 'researchers', i.e. scientists, have said that these things are TRUE. Are they having a laugh?

Beer can increase your ability to make rational decisions. Seriously. So next time you grab your keys at the end of a long sesh, screech out of the pub car park and into a lurking police car, you can explain to the unhappy officer that you were following the advice of Canadian researchers who claimed that your decision-making was improved by drinking beer.

Students! **BEER MAKES YOU BRAINY**. 'Researchers' (yes, them again) claim that people who consumed anywhere between one and 30 (like the scale!) drinks a week were brainier in tests than teetotallers ... stick that in your pint of Why?

Beer Drinkers will eventually become immortal. 'Research' shows that beer makes your heart fitter by stretching your arteries, which means you live longer and can drink more. Which means Beer Drinkers **WILL RULE THE WORLD**. Your round, I think ...

What's more, Italian researchers say that beer stops you going to the shops in your pyjamas when you're older. You can stay in the pub, alert, suave and sophisticated, while the abstemious ones get carted off to the Piss and Dribble Home.

Beer keeps you regular. Two pints contain twenty per cent of your required daily fibre intake. You can get ahead by drinking ten pints a day.

Real ales contain Vitamin B, which will combat the effects of alcohol – **IT ACTUALLY STOPS YOU GETTING A HANGOVER!**

As we sit here and write this, our rational decision-making is also being improved. Cheers.

Pint trivia

Did you know? No, of course you didn't; but then neither did we ... so here it is.

Beer words and phrases

Did you know that when you describe something as 'ropey' or use a 'rule of thumb' you are using brewing words?

Ropey – if you think something is not up to scratch then you may call it 'a bit shit' or 'ropey'. That comes from strands of bacteria floating in infected beer – fit only for the drain or the Stella pump.

Rule of Thumb – before brewers had a thermometer to check the temperature at different stages of the brewing process, they used to stick their thumb in to see whether the brew was at the right level. This was called the 'rule of thumb'.

Mind Your Ps and Qs – We have it on good authority (see *Talking Shit*, page 107) that the 'Ps and Qs' in question are pints and quarts. When things got a bit messy after three solid days drinking at your 18th-century hostelry, the landlord would shout 'Mind your pints and quarts' as a way of reminding his faithful (if completely oblivious) customers that, if they were too rowdy, they might spill their drink.

Three Sheets to the Wind – is a sailor's expression, from the days of sailing ships. The terminology of sailing ships is excessively complicated and, every time I refer to it, people say I've got it wrong, usually contradicting each other. So treat what follows as a broad-brush treatment, open to dispute on the fine points. We ignorant landlubbers might think that a sheet is a sail, but, in traditional sailing-ship days, a *sheet* was a rope, particularly one attached to the bottom corner of a sail (it actually comes from an Old English term for the corner of a sail). The sheets were vital, since they trimmed the sail to the wind. If they ran loose, the sail would flutter about in the wind and the ship would wallow off its course out of control.

Extend this idea to sailors on shore leave, staggering back to the ship after a good night on the town, well tanked up. The irregular and uncertain locomotion of these jolly tars must have reminded onlookers of the way a ship, on which the sheets were loose, moved. Perhaps one loose sheet might not have been enough to get the image across, so the speakers borrowed the idea of a three-masted sailing ship with three sheets loose, so the saying became *three sheets to the wind*.

The Hair of the Dog (that bit you) – in Scotland (naturally) it was a popular and convenient belief that a few hairs of the dog that bit you applied to the wound would prevent evil consequences. Happily this translated to drinks – so if you have indulged too freely, take a glass of the same poison the next morning to soothe the nerves.

Chunder – there are lots of theories on this one. (One is that when someone was being sick on the upper deck of an emigrant ship, they'd shout out 'Watch under' but, lacking time, it became abbreviated to 'chunder'. Sadly not true.) It probably originates from a cartoon strip in Australia published around the time of the First World War called Chunder Loo. The name became rhyming slang for 'spew'. Barry Humphries made it popular in the UK in the 60s.

Honeymoon – The accepted practise in Babylon, 4000 years ago was for the bride's father to supply the groom with a month's supply of beer after the wedding. This was based on the lunar calendar, therefore, Honeymoon. And a perfect reason to get down to action right away. To the beer, I mean ... THE BEER!

The Gods of beer

'Beer is proof that God loves us.'

Benjamin Franklin

It's a rite of passage to pray to the porcelain God. Long before the toilet was invented, though, beer was produced in ancient cultures around the world. Naturally there exists a pubful of deities to worship for bringing the golden nectar to humankind. Here's our guide to the holiest of holy spirits:

1 DIONYSUS (Ancient Greece)
Dionysus is the God of Sex and Intoxicating Drinks – brilliant. The son of big-daddy god Zeus. He shagged everything in sight and drank for Greece, and then Rome where he had become 'Bacchus', and inspired the drunken orgy. What a bloke!

2 SILENUS (Ancient Greece)
Fat, bald with a huge beer belly, Silenus is the God of Beer and drinking companions. Impressively, tutored top god Dionysus in the arts of debauchery. When leathered, Silenus possessed special powers including prophecy, but who doesn't?

3 NINKASI (Mesopotamia)
Ninkasi is the Ancient Sumerian Goddess of booze and human desire. It is said this lovely lady provided the world with the secret to make beer. Her name means 'the lady who fills the mouth'. Yes really! A Sumerian poet wrote the Hymn to Ninkasi in 1800 BC, which includes one of the first recipes for brewing beer (see page 41).

4 AEGIR (Scandinavia)

The Norse God of the Ocean and Beer. Sea froth is the head from his underwater brewery, where he would drag sailors and ships. There they discovered Aegir put on a great party – beer just poured itself. Wrote 'In the Navy' with the Village People.

5 TEZCATZONTECATL (Aztec)

Tezcatzontecatl (try saying that after ten pints) is the Aztec God of pulque, or Aztec beer. Pulque was hallucinogenic, prompting lesser gods to give up work and form a group called The Infinite Rabbits. We'll stick to the proper ale, thanks. He is also god of drunkenness and fertility, which as we know go together only too well.

6 MBABA MWANA WARESA (Africa)

In Zulu mythology, Mbaba Mwana Waresa is the Goddess of beer. She is also known as the Goddess of rain and produces rainbows at times of celebration. One of the nicer Beer Gods, but there's not much competition.

7 YASIGI (Africa)

In Dogon culture (Mali), Yasigi is the Goddess of beer, dance and masks, which might have been the forerunner of beer goggles. Statues of her show a huge-chested female dancing while holding a beer ladle. Where do we sign up?

MORRISSEY MAXIM

Like an exceptional ale, the best women need laying for a couple of months before they give of their best.

8 RAGUTIS, RAGUTIENE and RAUGUPATIS (Eastern Europe)

In Lithuania, Beer is so important it has not one, not two, but three Gods in charge. Ragutis is the God of Beer – the landlord. Ragutiene is the Goddess of beer – his wife. And Raugupatis is the God of Fermentation, the master brewer who brings it all together. Now that's what we call Eastern European organisation.

9 SHADIPINYI (Africa)

Shadipinyi is the evil Namibian God of drunken behaviour. He invented beer and gave it to mankind to get them in trouble. Worshippers of Shadipinyi fill city centres at the weekend, fighting and making pavement pizzas in his honour. Shadipinyi, you're one beer God we wish didn't exist.

10 GOIBHNIU (Ireland)

Also known in Wales as Gofannon, this Irish deity was an ancient smith god, making unbeatable swords. He also brewed an ale which made those who drank it immortal. So if you drank the beer before getting in a fight with someone who had one of his swords, everyone got confused. Typical. Anyway cheers, or sláinte!

11 OSIRIS (Eygpt)

Osiris is the God of Agriculture, Beer and the Underworld. In ancient Egypt they knew beer. Beer was food. Everyone was paid in beer. Even the dead were given beer to help them on their journey to the to the Underworld where Osiris was waiting, with a beer lined up of course. Ancient Egypt – pissed-up big time.

Earliest beer recipe

The earliest known recipe was discovered recently. It's for beer, it's over 5,000 years old and it's written like a hymn. Well, fuck my old boots off – that is great.

The Hymn to Ninkasi...

You are the one who waters the malt set on the ground,
The noble dogs keep away even the potentates,
You are the one who soaks the malt in a jar,
The waves rise, the waves fall.
You are the one who spreads the cooked mash on large reed mats,
Coolness overcomes,
You are the one who holds with both hands the great sweet wort,
Brewing [it] with honey [and] wine
(You the sweet wort to the vessel)
The filtering vat, which makes a pleasant sound,
You place appropriately on a large collector vat.
When you pour out the filtered beer of the collector vat,
It is [like] the onrush of Tigris and Euphrates.

Beer

☞ Drinking

The Pub

Food

Drinking your pint

We've looked at the beautiful liquid, now what about the beautiful act? Drinking has its own rituals, language, romance, heroes and games. This section is all about the BEAUTY OF DRINKING.

Beer, as someone should have said, is the backbone of the nation – we are a nation of pissheads, always have been, always will be. The degree of our pissheadedness has shocked most visitors to these islands for many centuries. Why else do we have hundreds of words for being off our tits? But, do you know what? Who cares? We're always up for a good night out and that usually involves pints galore. Here is Morrissey and Foxy's very own guide to Drinking.

First, let's acknowledge that people in other countries do drink – they have their habits and their modest targets; they have 'sophisticated' café culture and they practise restraint. They even have some words to begin drinking with – their equivalent of our 'cheers' (*see over*). Here are some of the phrases shouted worldwide when the drink starts to flow, then some expressions for when it has really flowed and then some others for when it has really overflowed ...

MORRISSEY MAXIM

*Never drink more than
your age in pints.*

Multi-lingual cheers

'Aish Karo!' *Enjoy!* – India • **'Be Salamati!'** – Iran • **'Budmo!'** *Shall we live forever!* Usually one person says 'Budmo!' and everybody in the group reponds – Ukraine • **'Bunden i vejret eller resten i håret'** *Bottoms up or the rest in your hair* – Denmark • **'Cin cin'** – Italy **'Tin tin'** – Brazil • **'Egészségedre!'** *To your good health!* – Hungary **'Geiá mas'** *Our health!* – Greece • **'Gesondheid'** – Afrikaans **'Iechyd Da'** – Wales • **'Jamas Gia'sou'** – Greece • **'Kanpai'** – Japan **'Kassutta'** – *Let our glasses meet* • **'Imeqatigiitta'** – *Let's drink together* **'Kasugta'** – Greenland • **'Kippis'** – Finland • **'L'Chaim'** – Jewish **'Letenachin'** – Ethiopia (vulgar apparently) • **'Nastravé!'** *Help* – Bulgaria • **'Na zdrowie'** *to health* – Poland • **'Noroc!'** *Good luck!* – Romania • **'Nush'** *Enjoy it, and let it be part of your body* – Persia (Iran) **'Okole maluna Okole malune Hipahipa'** – Hawaii • **'Proost'** – The Netherlands • **'Prost'** – Germany and German-speaking places **'Saliq!'** – Azerbaijan • **'Salud'** – Spain • **'Salut!'** or **'Salut i Forca al Canut'** – Catalan • **'Salute'** or **'alla salute'**, **'Prosit'**; **'Sănătate!'** *To (your) good health!* – Romania • **'Santé'**, **'Chin'**, or **'Tchin Tchin'** – France and Québec • **'Sant Hilari, fill de puta qui no se l'acabi'** *Son of bitch, the one that does not finish the cup* – Spain • **'Saúde'** – Portugal and Lusophone countries • **'Schol'** – Flanders • **'Şerefe'** – Turkey **'Skál'** – Iceland • **'Skål'** – Denmark, Norway, Sweden and parts of Finland • **'Sláinte'** – Ireland and among Scots Gaelic speakers **'Topa!'** *Meet the glasses!* – Basque • **'Wihayeo'** – Korea • **'Yung sing'** *Drink and win* – Chinese • **'Gan bei'** or **'Gom bui'** *Dry the cup* – Cantonese • **'За вас!'** – Russia, generic toast, in English often spelled 'Za vas', meaning *to you*; **'За прекрасных дам!'** – *To beautiful ladies!*

Not a bad effort, but we British are the only ones to do this important ritual justice. Here are just some of the words and phrases we use every day.

Pint 1: 'Cheers'

Pint 2: 'Good health'

Pint 3: 'Down the hatch'

Pint 4: 'Bottoms up'

Pint 5: 'In for a penny, in for a pound'

Pint 6: 'Nice one'

Pint 7: 'To you, mate – no seriously, what could be better than sitting with your mate in the pub'

Pint 8: 'I have it on good authority…'
(see *Talking Shit*, page 107)

Pint 9: 'She looks tasty'

Pint 10: 'What about a little chaser?'

Pint 11: 'Ralph…'

Pint 12: 'Ugh'

The Navy has played a part in giving us good cheers expressions. When 'recruitment officers' toured the pubs in Portsmouth, they dropped a shilling in men's pints; if the man drank the pint, they were supposed to have taken 'the king's shilling' and joined up. In those days, pint pots had glass bottoms, so 'bottoms up' (i.e. raising the glass to look at it from underneath to check whether there was a shilling in the bottom) was a way of making sure you didn't end up at the Battle of Trafalgar.

The A–Z of bollocksed

Another way we Brits excel over all other nations is because we have literally hundreds of ways of saying 'I'm drunk'. Impressively, there is a list of over 800 words and phrases for excess but here is Morrissey and Foxy's personal selection of ways to describe being utterly bollocksed.

12 gauged · Ankled · **Annihilated** · Armchaired
Banjoed · Badgered · **Banjaxed** · Battered · **Befuggered**
Bernhard Langered · **Bevvied** · Blackboarded (for teachers)
Bladdered · Blasted · **Blathered** · Bleezin · **Blitzed**
Blootered · **Blottoed** · Bluttered · **Boogaloo**
Boiled as an owl · Brahms & Liszt · **Buckled** · Burlin
Cabbaged · Chevy Chased · **Clobbered** · Chateaued
Decimated · Dot Cottoned · **Druck-steaming**
Drunk as a lord · **Drunk as a skunk**
De-ossified · **Drunk uncle** · Etched
Fecked · Fleemered · **Four to the floor**
Fuggled · **Full tight** · Full of loud mouth soup
Gatted · Goosed · **Got my beer goggles on**
Guttered · **Gibbled** · Had a couple of shickers
Hammer-blowed · Hammered · **Hanging**
Having a close look at the footpath
Having the whirligigs · HowlingI · **In the paint**
Inebriated · **Intoxicated** · Jahalered
Jaiked up · Jan'd (abbrev for) Jan Hammered
Jaxied · Jeremied · **Jolly Jagged up jackassed**
Juice-looped · **Jober as a Sudge** · Kaned
Kennedied · Lagged up · **Lamped**
Langered (Ireland) [also langers, langerated] · **Laroped, or alt. larrupt**
Lashed · **Leathered** · Legless · **Lightulbed** · Liquored up
Locked · Locked out of your mind (Ireland) · **Loo la liver-lubed**
Mad wey it · **Mandoo-ed** · Mangled · **Manky** · Mashed

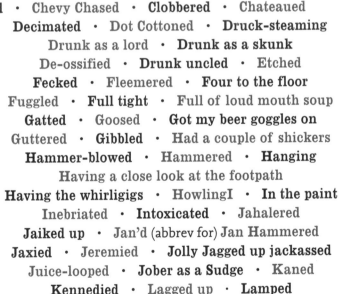

Meff'd · Merl Haggard · **Merry** · Michael Fished
Minced · Ming-ho · **Minging** · Ming mong · **Moired**
Monged · **Monkey-full** · Mothered · **Mottled** · Mullahed
Monkey assed · Mullocked · **Mullered** · Newcastled
Nicely irrigated with horizontal lubricant · **Off the leash**
One over the eight · **Off me pickle** · Off me trolley
On a campaign · Out of it · **Out yer tree** · Paggered
Palintoshed · **Paraletic** · Pavement Diving · **Peelywally**
Peevied · Pickled · **Pie-eyed**
Pile-axed · **Pished** · Plastered
Poleaxed · Pollatic paralytic
Picassoed · **Pixelated**
Predicting earthquakes · Rat-assed
Rat-legged (Stockport) · **Ratted**
Ravaged · Razzled · **Reek-ho**
Refreshed · **Rendered** · Rosy glow
Rubbered · Ruined · **Shined up**
Skinned · **Slaughtered** · Stinko
Swipey · Saying hello to Mr Armitage
Sauted · Scattered · **Schindlers**
Screwed · **Scuttered** · Shedded – as in
My shed has collapsed taking most of the fence with it · **Slaughtered**
Sloshed · **Smashed** · Snatered · **Snobbled** · Sozzled
Spangled · Spannered · **Spiffed** · Spongelled · **Squiffy**
Steamin · **Steampigged** · Stewed · **Stocious** · Stonkin
Torn off the frame · **Tabled** · Tanked · **Tashered**
Tipsy · **Trashed** · Trollied · **Troubled** · Trousered
Tulipped · Twisted · **Two rounds with** [add appropriate boxer]
Torqued · **Troll-eyed** · Tired and emotional · **Thora-Hirded**
Warped · Wasted · **Wearing the wobbly boot** · Wellied
With the fairies · **Wrecked** · Wired to the tits · **Wankered**
Wearing a big hat · **Wingdinged** · Wallsliding
Zigzag · Zombied

In fact, if you take any word and add '–ed' to the end, it works.

'I can't come into work today because I have ...'

Here are a few of the words and phrases in the language of the hangover worldwide:

Katzenjammer
– a wailing of kittens (Germany)

Ont I haret
– a pain in the roots of the hair (Sweden)

The Tommermen
– the lumberjacks in the head (Norway)

Futsuka yoi
– a two-day hangover (Japan – a heroic effort)

Crudo – raw (Mexico)

And, in English:

Divine punishment (if on a Sunday)
Brown bottle flu
Suffering the wrath of grapes
Wearing loud shoes
Red-eyed and bushy-tongued
Post-refreshment syndrome

Eight types of drunkard

by **Thomas Nashe** [with slightly updated spelling]

Research into drinking has been going on for centuries. In the 1500s Thomas Nashe identified eight types of drunk – a piece of work that is entirely in keeping with the spirit of this book.

Nor have we one or two kinde of drunkards only, but eight kinds. The first is **Ape drunk**, and he leaps, and sings, and hollows, and dances for the heauens: the second is **Lion drunk**, and he flings the pots about the house, calls his Hostess whore, breaks the glass windows with his dagger, and is apt to quarrel with any man that speaks to him: the third is **Swine drunk**, heavy, lumpish, and sleepy, and cries for a little more drink, and a few more clothes: the fourth is **Sheep drunk**, wise in his own conceit, when he cannot bring forth a right word, the fifth is **Maudlin drunk**, when a fellow will weep for kindnes in the midst of his Ale, and kiss you, saying; by God Captain I love thee, go thy ways thou dost not think so often of me as I do of thee, I would (if it pleased GOD) I could not love thee so well as I do, and then he puts his finger in his eye, and cries: the sixth is **Martin drunke**, when a man is drunk and drinks himself sober ere he stirs: the seventh is Goat drunk, when in his drunkenness he hath no mind but on Lechery: the eighth is **Fox drunk**, when he is crafty drunk, as many of the Dutch men be, will never bargain but when they are drunke. All these *Species* and more I have seen practised in one Company at one sitting, when I have beene permitted to remain sober amongst them, only to note their several humours. He that plies any one of them harde, it will make him to write admirable verses, to have a deepe casting head, though he were never so very a Dunce before.

If you're any of the above, it's likely that you have staggered into the loo and changed into a man of iron and steel with all the powers of a **GOD**. You are on the Top Shelf.

The Top Shelf

SuperDrunk (see page 54) always visits the Top Shelf. He is blissfully unaware of the hushed tones of other punters in the pub as he shouts for his Top Shelf poison of choice. But there are some places and occasions in pubs where the red neon sign is on and it's flashing DANGEROUS. Be afraid, be very afraid. The Top Shelf needs study; the Top Shelf is a rare and exotic place; the Top Shelf is beautifully dangerous ... Remember Icarus? He did the mythological equivalent of reaching for the Top Shelf without due care and attention and look what happened to him. The Top Shelf has also had a massive impact on history:

Knock in Ireland as a place of pilgrimage. Actually it was inspired by a rare local potsheen – while we admire the fact that the Virgin Mary spotters kept their drinking regional (no Potsheen Miles there), we question the validity of the sighting after a vat of Lethal Potato Brew.

Appointment of Steve McClaren as England manager. The FA must have had a long day and night visiting the Board Room Top Shelf. How else can you explain it?

The shape of (the country) Jordan. Winston Churchill lived most of his life on the Top Shelf. He even had brandy brought to him in bed while he was dictating important political things. At some conference or other, deciding the allocation of territory in the Middle East, he was allegedly drawing a straight line for the border of Jordan and apparently he sneezed. The line jagged out but our Winston refused to acknowledge his error – probably having been on the Top Shelf most of the day and feeling a bit like Superman. And that's how Jordan got its shape – because of the Top Shelf. How Jordan the well-known novelist and mother got her shape we won't discuss here for legal reasons.

Van Gogh's ear. Vincent liked a bit of Top Shelf action.

Napoleon's march. What the fuck was he thinking? This was late night on the brandy. At that point most of us think we can leap cars; not Napoleon – oh, no, the Top Shelf made him think he was a GOD. He could march through Russia in the middle of winter because he was TOP SHELF INVINCIBLE.

Rasputin. A Top Shelf Merchant. See also Boris Yeltsin below. Russia seems to have had more than its fair share of Top Shelfers. Rasputin survived three attempts to rub him out. Some said it was the Devil that kept him alive; we know he hit Top Shelf Nirvana – he and the vodka were wedded in spiritual understanding.

The Sinclair C-5. Surely the only explanation?

The DeLorean. A C-5 moment with knobs on.

Synchronised swimming. Not to be mistaken for a game of pool. (See *Things Not to Do When Drunk*, page 58.)

Boris Yeltsin. A fine exponent of the Top Shelf. Boris climbed on a tank to find the nearest bar when he beat some other politicians who were trying to overthrow his mate, Mikhail 'Dodgy Blotch on Head' Gorbachev. When he became President, he was often 'unavailable' during state visits. He died in 2007. When his friends and family and allies gathered for a wake to commemorate his life, his widow said that this was 'how Boris would have wanted to be remembered, if he'd ever been sober enough to state a preference'. Blood alcohol tests showed that, even though the event took place five days after his death, Mr Yeltsin was still the most pissed person at the event. There is a brand of vodka named after him. Without the Top Shelf, Russia would be a very different place today. If he'd been a beer rather than vodka drinker he would have made Beer Hero status.

George W. Bush. A reformed Top Shelfer but perhaps living 40 per cent proof that, once you get there, you should stay there for the good of mankind (oh, and the ladies as well).

The whole of California had been on the Top Shelf when they voted Arnie Schwarzenegger in.

Finally, you know that when you walk into some pubs there are certain people who you know are simply **BAD NEWS**. Quite often, you can see them with a short glass in front of them. It is a maxim of ours that you should always, always **BEWARE THE TOP SHELF STARTER**. This is the bloke who has been there, done that and heads straight for the optics. He is trouble. If you find yourself at the bar with him, heed the words of the late, lamented Michael Elphick: 'You can drink in my company, but don't try and drink with me.' The Top Shelf Starter is someone to watch, not someone to mimic. There is a place people go above the Top Shelf. Known as The Attic, this is the darkened room where drinkers stop before checking out altogether. If you get there you won't be aware of it but things such as vodka snorting and brandy inhaling are common. If you're there you're beyond any kind of hope and there you'll stay until your own closing time.

A tour of the Top Shelf spiritual home ...

So take a trip with us, a trip out on the edge – we'll try and stop you falling. With the Landlord as your shaman, let's meet the Top Shelf family.

Gin. The Daddy of the shelf. A sophisticated spirit as at home with an olive as a low-calorie tonic. Quite a good way to kick off the evening if you're in serious shape. Mixes well, doesn't tolerate abuse, though has a history of causing mayhem in public places. Calmed his act down and is now more likely to be seen at the theatre than down Gin Lane.

Vodka. The Hard Man. Top Shelf mate of those who don't want their 'visits' known about. A real bad boy who will be there for you first thing in the morning, all afternoon and well into the night, no questions asked. Do you want him there that much? If you do, you'd better shout 'Help' from the Top Shelf. He's not gonna make it easy to get back down. Can be quite refreshing once in a while with grapefruit or orange juice, we're told.

Whisky. Also Well Hard, but more in your face – think Robert Carlyle in *Trainspotting*; think juiced-up Jocks rampaging over Wembley's hallowed turf. A nice companion to that Last Orders pint but best not to take the bottle home unless you want things to get messy.

Single Malts. The educated cousin of whisky, the Single Malt is a glorious spirit. The style of a SM is affected by many factors including the barley, yeast and water used, and the process of maturation. Entertaining and urbane on its own, not likely to be necked at pace and, unlike its rough and ready-blended brother, the Single Malt is rather sniffy about some of its Top Shelf companions.

Liqueurs. The girl's Top Shelf, with a few cross-dressers for the desperate man trying to pull a spirit. How many of these do you have lurking at the back of your closet? Cherry Brandy, Tia Maria, Bailey's Cream? Cointreau, Southern Comfort and Drambuie are a bit more like it, but pretty soft next to the rest of the family. Southern Comfort is actually a peach liqueur – not a lot of people know that.

Vermouth. Or, as we know it in Britain, Cinzano. Good in company, mixes particularly well with Big Daddy gin and Hard Man vodka, but a bit of a slut on her own. Has a thing about schoolboys.

Brandy. His Imperial Majesty of spirits in the right setting but, encountered in pubs, is more likely to be a pauper pretending to be a king. The con man with a suitcase full of bricks and the deeds to the vomitorium: 'Just sign here, old chap!'

Rum. Laid-back Caribbean fantasies are conjured up in marketing campaigns, but there's a wicked uncle lurking in the bottle. Hearty fun with cola and company, but get him on his own and you might regret it.

Tequila. The Devil's own top-up, distilled from cactus. It's a fun and creative way to pass out, or to end up sleeping on top of a cupboard with a nose full of salt.

Schnapps. The strict Teutonic Aunt of ze Top Shelf (quite a hottie, truth be told). Click those heels and dream of home. Flavoured with aniseed or caraway, and mostly popular with our North European brethren. Highly unlikely to be making an appearance in your local – at least until we get the Euro.

SuperDrunk

(Ladies, look away now.)

It's half past seven. A good time. A decent time. You and your best mate push open the hostelry door and are met by a warm, welcoming tide of sounds and sensations. Laughter and convivial chat fill the air and a fire crackles in the corner, imparting a golden glow across the walls.

Your saliva glands kick in as you walk to the bar – a length of pristine oak displaying a bewitching variety of brews. There's a new guest ale – must give it a try! You can see the Top Shelf glinting up above, and a heavyweight selection of single malts and quality vodkas on offer to those sad folks of weakened resolve. Sad, who needs it? As you peruse the pumps you sample the enticing bar snacks, thoughtfully laid out to whet the appetite. Delicious!

As the first mouthful of cool, hoppy beer slides down your throat you turn to your mate and smile. This is what it's all about! Friday night. On the town. A few quality beers, some good-natured banter, a release from the worries of the world. Later, maybe a curry and a DVD back at home, sound sleep and up for the joys of the weekend. Maybe a match? Maybe back here to watch the rugby? For now you can sink back and let the pub take the strain …

... So you're standing at the bar, 14 pints in. You need a slash, there's already a stain on your crotch from your last attempt. When you look around, things move too quickly, or at least more quickly than you. Crisp bits hang off your face, your eyes are bloodshot and your hair is like matted grease. Your breath stinks of yeasty swill, there is a pleasant bubbling in your bum and your hands are sticky from God knows what.

You are gorgeous! You can do anything! You are SuperDrunk! That beautiful woman keeps giving you the eye – you know what she's after. You smile at her seductively. She's looking away coyly. Women! What a tease!

Your mate doesn't look too good. In fact, shit, he looks AWFUL. Wait a minute, that's you ... oh, there's your mate. Jesus. The state of him. Some people don't know when they've had enough. Talking of which – oh, it's closing time, get them in. Top Shelf time. 'And a woman chaser!' Why can't the barman hear you? 'A whisky chaser!' Cheers.

That woman's leaving with her mate. What a hint. Easy to see where this is going. You head for the toilets, assume the one-arm brace (see *How to Drain the Lizard When Pissed as a Newt*, page 61) and piss for England. Quick glance in the mirror, wipe the crisps off your face and run wet hands through your hair. Now you wash them under the tap and do the same again. Go on – the smile. That's it: a bit crooked, mysterious, alluring, sexxxy. Your mate's being sick – there's no time for that. Grab him, wipe his mouth on your jacket and give him a gentle slap. 'Come on! We're in!' 'Where? What?' You laugh – what a mate!

Outside there's no sign of the ladies. This is bad news, they must have misread your signal. Their loss. There will be other women. Tonight. You feel your powers reviving in the cold air.

Ahead a brick wall bars your path to freedom, well, out of the pub car park. But you are SuperDrunk and nothing gets in your way. With a few bounds you are there, and a leap takes you up, up and not quite over the wall. Your face slams the concrete. It will not give. You slump to the floor. The need to piss is strong again. Maybe you can piss the wall away. You take aim at a gap in the concrete, trying to widen it with your golden, hot superpiss.

Behind you you hear giggling – like a silver brook. It's the ladies! They're still here! Excellent! Better play hard to get and zip up, even though you haven't finished. Your mate's being sick again, over a Vauxhall Astra. This is going to be up to you. Summoning all your super powers, you cross to meet them. My God, she's beautiful, even more beautiful than you remember eight pints ago, when you first exchanged glances. She was a bit of a munter then. Funny how wrong you can be. Her mate's not bad either – is a threesome on the cards? Nah, don't be greedy.

'Icouldn'thelpnoticingyouearlier,' you say, you think. 'Fuck off, you alky perv,' says the Dream Girl. 'Look, he's pissed himself.'

You laugh along with the banter, draw yourself to your full height and blow chunks all over her mate. You can tell she wasn't expecting that. SuperDrunk triumphs again.

The moral of this story? When you've got the Drink On, a clear head and the best intentions won't stop you coming home with a brain that's been tied in a sack and drowned in a river of beer. But, if you can't fool anyone else, at least you can fool yourself! Nice one SuperDrunk!

The beer drinker's guide to romance and seduction

On the other hand, in moderation, beer can be a very seductive drink. Oh yes, if you want to pull, get the intended victim down the pub; if she wants to taste your beer, you're in. It's time to shout loudly to the lads that there's a programme on TV that you just have to catch – about nine o'clock should get the maximum jealousy from them. If she doesn't taste your beer but seems up for it, then think before you slide down the slippery beer slope. The Department for Total Pissheads has produced this authoritative graph, which measures seduction ability, actual performance and perceived performance in both areas against number of pints drunk.

Number of pints

There are some important points on this graph.

Perceived resurgence of performance at about eight pints – that's the point at which you become the Superman of Love; the red pants and cape come out in the loo and you stride back in to the pub ready for **LURV.**

The seduction line goes down dramatically at the point at which you start fancying other women and goes off the scale when you start fancying your mate.

Perception is the key measure: just look at yourself in the mirror after eight pints and you'll think your name is **THE LOVE GOD**.

If things are going well but she's going to take a bit more convincing check out the romantic beer dinner recipes beginning on page 126.

Things not to do when drunk

So, you've got the wobbly boot on and everything looks rosy. You've been to the Top Shelf in an invigorating way and you're SuperDrunk. Any number of things can now happen; most of them are to be avoided. The line 'It seemed like a good idea at the time' is one of the saddest in the English language. In such circumstances, you should have all of this advice in your head because 'a good idea at the time' is not the language of success – it is the language of regret. Do not do any of the following:

- **Text someone you may have a sober chance of a liaison with** – particularly not at 10.45 p.m. when you're getting the last round in (which only too often includes a visit to the Top Shelf).

- **Text ex-girlfriends** – ever; but particularly after 16 pints.

- **Make excuses when you get home** – no matter how convincing they are to your mates or in your head, they just won't wash as you fumble the keys and walk into the kitchen table.

- **Tell her how much you love her** – on the phone, from the pub, repeatedly. Under no circumstances get your mates to tell her how much you love her either – unlike football players, women don't seem to enjoy mass chanting of their name ...

- **Go fishing** – rods, big fish, water. No.

- **Go swimming** – or, worse, body-surfing off an unknown beach in any kind of oceans that might contain large aggressive beasts. You don't know what the fuck's in the sea and you don't know how strong the undertow is. You may well have been drinking a local brew that makes you feel even more like Superman than normal.

☞ Get things out of other people's eyes – get a professional or tell the person to go to bed. If it's a lady, don't suggest you take her. It's just a bad chat-up line.

☞ Play Scrabble – you'll fall asleep and it'll be a real downer.

☞ Light farts – not only hazardous, but quite smelly.

☞ Engage policemen in conversation – they don't think you're funny when you're sober.

☞ Direct traffic – see policemen above.

☞ Exercise bladder relief – anywhere but officially designated toilets.

☞ Any kind of jumping – see *SuperDrunk*, page 54.

☞ Hang out with Amy Winehouse – the Top Shelf and The Attic beckon.

☞ Use bad chat-up lines – in fact don't try any chat-up lines – the very sight of your slobbering mouth and roaming eyes will make even the very best, Richard Gere-inspired line sound like 'Fancy a shag' as uttered by Peter Beardsley.

☞ Approach celebrities – they (sorry, we) don't like it and we have better lawyers than you.

☞ Try to kiss your new girlfriend after you and God have had a conversation on the Great White Telephone – (even if you have used the chewable toothbrush). Instead, have a small whisky, gargle, clean up meticulously and, if you can see the right mouth, go for it.

☞ Do backward-standing somersaults – slightly obscure, maybe, but sound advice nonetheless as a friend will testify. He would often perform this trick after seven too many. You'd be standing with him at a party and, if he looked over his shoulder, you just knew it was going to happen. He'd say, 'Hold my pint', and then, whomph, he'd do his piece, rebalance and take his pint back. One time, he did it, and, whack, he cracked his head on something. Said he was fine, we carried on. Walking back from the party, he said, 'You know what? It's bleeding a bit now.' He felt his head and there was blood, so we swung by A&E – he didn't come out for six weeks. Went into a coma. So, no backward-standing somersaults.

- **Anything that is 'a good idea at the time'** – no.

- **Join the army or any other organisation** – much as you convince yourself that becoming a Scout Leader would be a worthy thing to do and would 'put something back into the community', in the morning you'll find that it is the exclusive domain of Geography and Games teachers and that you are now expected to wear a woggle and a beige uniform on a Friday night. 'The few, the proud, the geeky' as Lisa Simpson once described them.

- **Test how hard a punch you can take** – Do not try to get into this game especially with strangers – it hurts.

- **Make bets – or dares** – two slightly different things going on here. The rule of being hustled is that if someone comes over and makes a bet with you, generally speaking you're going to lose. If you succumb to accepting a dare, you're in 'Seemed like a good idea at the time' territory. And that's a dangerous place.

- **Light matches on the heads of people you don't know** – particularly if they are bald, have intense eyes and are surrounded by 'friends' in suits. What they lack in a sense of humour they make up for in ways of inflicting pain.

- **Finally, under no circumstances commit acts of pure financial bravado** – buying everyone in the pub a drink won't make you any more friends but it *will* make you broke. Keep the plastic in your pocket if you're tempted to hit the Top Shelf – no matter how much you love the world, your life and the barmaid.

If you are capable of any of the above – go to rehab as soon as possible.

As an aside, here are some things not to take out with you if you know you might be a while: knife; swimming trunks; sunglasses; fishing rod; girlfriend – and anything you want with you the next morning should be clipped on (particularly if starting on a summer afternoon).

How to drain the lizard when pissed as a newt

Before you go car-jumping, knocking policemen's helmets off or whatever insane post-pub activity your addled brain lands on, you need to give the old bladder a break. With the wobbly boot, this is not as easy as it should be. Luckily we have a handy guide to draining the lizard when you're well and truly badgered.

1. Sit down,
you know it makes sense.

2. Head rest.
Makes aim better and reduces trouser splash.

3. One-arm brace.
Has the added advantage of being in a good
position if Ralph and Huey come to call.

4. Get someone to hold you.
But only if you know them really well and they aren't
more bladdered than you. Struggling on the floor of the
Gents with your mate at closing time is not a good look.

How to deal with drunks

For a moment, let's forget that you've had eight pints and look at it from another angle. If you have to deal with the Top Shelfer slumped in the corner, what do you do without getting a slap?

Here is Morrissey's top tip for handling those people who just don't know they've had enough. We've all been there. The bloke in the corner can't see his pint, let alone his hand, but he refuses to go. Can't see what the problem is and could get a bit lairy if you suggest he goes one more time. Things could get messy if you touch him in any way.

Best way to deal with him is this. Say, 'Your taxi will be here in ten minutes.' He'll object and say, 'I don't want a fucking taxi, I want another pint (or perhaps something from the Top Shelf).' Walk away. You've planted the seed of 'easy way to get home'. Ten minutes later, wander over and say, 'Your taxi's here, mate.' He'll say, 'Oh, cheers, nice one. See ya,' and can be either escorted to the door or allowed to make his own way there. Works with everyone.

MORRISSEY MAXIM

*The Friday Night Thirst
is a Monster in Disguise –
treat with caution.*

The multi-coloured
pavement pizza

Later, or during the following day, as you heave the night's consumption into a suitable receptacle (Neil's top tip: if outside, face away from the wind), think of the following:

Air the diced carrots · Backwards bungee jumping
Barf · Blow your biscuits · **Call the crows**
Call God on the great white telephone
Chunder · **Deliver a pizza** · Feed your young
Fertilise the sidewalk · **Fling floor pie**
Front door diarrhoea · Have an exorcist moment
Hiccup from hell · Hurl · **Kebab on the rebound**
Laughing all over your shoes · **Liquid laughing**
Losing calories · Lose your lunch
Out of stomach experience · **Pray to the porcelain god**
Ralph and Huey · Reverse drinking
Review the last meal · **Savoury milkshake**
Shout groceries · Soul coughing · **Stomach tsunami**
Sweet and sour flood · Train to be a super model
Upchuck · **Whistle beef**

Ugh and better ugh

'I was left in no doubt as to the severity of the hangover when the cat stamped into the room' PG Wodehouse

You're faced with the consequences of your actions: if your body were an animal it would be one of those extinct ones. Poor fucker, you are now in one of the following states. Here we present the Morrissey–Fox Hangover Scale.

You are in your own bed, a mild headache, no visible signs of body malfunction, just a slight throb in the eye perhaps. You got away with it. You are **Didn't Try Hard Enough Hungover**.

WORK: *Sadly, yes, but you can always claim that you're feeling 'slightly under the weather'.*

Swimming in a pool with Ralph and Huey, got a sticky eye and your clothes are only worth incinerating. Head: pounding but nothing that a couple of paracetamol won't cure. Legs: stiff from lying awkwardly wherever you collapsed. Mouth: a dead squirrel may have slept there but nothing that a few gargles won't deal with. Body: sweaty on the outside, cold on the inside. You are **Messy Hungover**, but at least the Vomit Monster has called and you don't have that ritual couple of hours facing the Great U-Bend to look forward to.

WORK: *Possible with due care and attention.*

Running to the toilet, holding your mouth, eyes popping. The other complication is that you don't know where the toilet is because this is not your home … You are **Lost Hungover**. You don't know where you are, your body doesn't know who you are and everything is alien. You're fucked. There are still a couple of hours of chundering to do, no home comforts to take the edge off things and the potential huge embarrassment of doing all of this in front of a Gnawer for whom you had the beer goggles on the night before. There is only one solution to this – don't try to find the bathroom, head for the front door and keep running.

WORK: *Nope. Not for a couple of days yet. Ring in with mystery virus, preferably in the middle of an awesome burst of carrot tossing.*

In your own bed, eyes tentatively opened and surprisingly little pain. You jump up with a smile on your face, thinking, 'Phew, got away with that, don't feel so bad. I must really be able to put it away these days …' Then you fall flat on your red face. Because you're still drunk. You are **Pissed Hungover**. It may be ten in the morning but it's still last night as far as your body is concerned. You can handle this in one of two ways:
i) decide that the only way is to keep your body unaware of the fact that it's morning and keep going until you fall asleep; OR
ii) take Ray Winstone's Preventative Hangover Cure (see overleaf) and retire to bed.

WORK: *Under no circumstances should you attempt to call or make contact. At the first available opportunity get a friend or partner to call in.*

In hospital – relax you're in the best possible place. Shout 'Nurse' and wait for the best possible painkillers to be gently introduced to your battered body. You are **Clinically Hungover**.

WORK: *Don't worry, as soon as you mention the word 'hospital' everyone stops listening to why you're there and concentrates on feeling sympathetic.*

There are gradations between these states, a sort of staggering scale, but these are the main staging posts along the way.

Hangover cures

There are some cures that people swear on their next pint by (and are actually as effective as a drunk in a brewery), and there are cures that actually do work (Ray Winstone, we are not worthy). For completeness's sake we also include frankly weird suggestions from people who have told us about these 'foolproof' methods over many years.

Cures

Ray Winstone says this cure has saved him from the great white telephone countless times. Take a sachet of rehydration salts, two ibuprofen and a pint of water. You'll come up smiling in the morning – rehydrated, with your minerals in balance and no headache. After countless pints and a trip to the Top Shelf, this is quite a menu to get together but, hey, nobody said it was going to be easy.

The classic Bloody Mary – you know the recipe, but did you know about adding a touch of sherry (over the back of a teaspoon) at the end of the mixing process? You drink the Bloody Mary through a sherry filter and all is right with the world. This has everything: vitamins, salts, whatever Tabasco does and the secret ingredient – booze. When you have a hangover, your brain swells, which gives you the headache; if you give it a little pep of booze then the brain will contract and the pain is eased. Do not operate heavy machinery with this cure.

The Surgeon Major – a glass of champagne, a splash of brandy, a couple of raw eggs ...

Go back to the comfort of your bed, pull up the duvet and only open your eyes again when you feel no pain. Roughly the same amount of time as you spent on the ale.

Worth a try

1. Those of you with a literary mind (like Dan Brown) might follow the Papillion remedy: lots of fresh, home-made orange juice (three oranges and one lemon mixed), a long shower and then loads of sex.

2. Coca-Cola can be used in initial stages to stop dysentery. So, after a particularly bad night on the curry or an especially dodgy kebab, it's exactly the thing. Has the binding qualities of a good boiled egg. Goodbye dribbly bottom.

3. Take a nice, long and hot sauna and follow up with a massage and spa.

4. Take premium PMS pills and they kick in within 20–25 minutes, apparently. They cure a headache, nausea, diarrhoea and light-headedness. Do so on the quiet, though. You don't want your mates finding out that you're taking girly stuff – and watch out for any developments in the chest area.

Complete bollocks or just bizarre

1. Burnt Toast: some people swear by this. But it's bollocks. It comes from a Victorian chimney-sweep urban myth – apparently they used to like soot mixed with milk to take away the effects of 80 per cent proof gin. Yeah, right.

2. Some blokes have claimed drinking a woman's breast milk cures hangovers after too many jugs … yeah, right.

3. People who believe in voodoo recommend sticking 13 black pins into the cork of the offending bottle.

4. Some foreigners insist you can cure the aftershocks by rubbing half a lemon under your 'drinking arm'. Clockwise in the Northern Hemisphere, anticlockwise in the Southern.

5. The Ancient Greeks believed that if you drank from amethyst cups it prevented you getting wasted … they should have stuck to philosophy and the Olympics.

6. Bitter almonds and raw eel was apparently very popular in the Middle Ages. Half the population also got wiped out by the plague. I think I'd rather be bitten by a rat than try this one.

7. The Coalman – melt some butter over a spoon into hot water, add a spoon of Worcestershire sauce and the same of orange juice, a pinch of cayenne pepper, half a glass of port (old, preferably). Soak some freshly made toast in the drink and eat the toast. Uh-huh.

8. Any animal part seems to have been suggested at some stage or other. Try any of these on their own or in a delicious reviving combination: horses' brains, dried rabbit droppings, raw owls' eggs, sheep lungs (apparently known as 'lights' to those in the know in Roman times), pickled sheeps' eye balls, ground swallow beaks (but only if mixed with myrrh), sheep's stomach soup.

If all else fails, call an ambulance and let the NHS take the strain.

Beer legends and heroes: we are not worthy

The Japanese actually have a word for a two-day hangover but most of us can only manage a session with consequences that reach into several days once in a while. Others can do this daily. Hats are being taken off and enthusiastically thrown in the air to the people below who we have called Beer Heroes.

There are two types of Beer Hero: there are people who have made the pint what it is today and who bring honour and respect to the business of brewing and drinking; then there are those who took it too far, and then a bit further, then they got stuck in. Some of them survived, some didn't. We celebrate here those people who demonstrate or have demonstrated dedication to the pint.

Beer legends

Martin Clunes – Beer god who helped a young nervous actor build up his resistance through the years. Thanks, matey.

Elizabeth I – Four pints at breakfast. Not bad for a posh girl.

Oliver Reed – The ultimate drinking man, but he really did like his ale. Legend has it that, during his stag weekend, Ollie downed 104 pints of beer. One-hundred-and-bloody-four! According to the groom, this beerfest took place 'during an arm-wrestling competition in Guernsey'. Where else? Oliver Reed, we salute you.

Peter O'Toole – Up there with Oliver Reed. A journalist from the *Daily Telegraph* said his habit was 'heavy drinking, even by heavy drinking standards'. This legend of stage, screen and umpteen bars has hundreds of drunken stories but he gets his beer wings for this quote alone: 'I drink now. But not like before. Christ, who could?'

Homer Simpson – Duff Beer's worst advert produced some of the best lines about booze: 'To alcohol: the cause of – and solution to – all of life's problems.' Hmmm.

Ernest Hemingway – Uniquely, perhaps, in American journalism, during the Second World War Hemingway managed to get himself a special alcohol ration so that he could drink himself to the margins of oblivion every day at the Paris Ritz. For getting the US government to recognise your needs, Ernest, we salute you.

Johnny Vegas – Jonny is a hero because he never appears on television or on the stage unless he's holding a beer. A permanent advert for alcohol consumption.

Bill Clinton – had a few beers in the Old Bell Tavern in Yorkshire and we can prove it because the spillage stain is still on the seat. An American with a penchant for a bit of a dark, warm brew.

Beer heroes

Peter Dowdeswell – The ultimate beer hero and a legend in speed beer drinking. Pete is the holder of 309 world records for drinking (and eating). Nice one, fella. His exploits have raised a mean £4.5 million for charity. This lad can down a pint in ⅖ths of a second, a pint *upside down* in one second and, get this, 90 pints of beer in three hours! Freakily, he doesn't drink … a night out with the missus for Pete is an orange juice and a packet of nuts. For your dedication to our cause, Pete, we salute you.

Alewives – These ladies invented the pub! They were the wives of farm workers in ye olde England who stayed at home brewing beer while the lads were out working the land. (We'll avoid making the obvious joke here for fear of never having sex again.) The house of the alewife who produced the best beer was where everyone went at the end of the day, making it a *public house*.

Ray Winstone – Cos of who he is and the hangover cure (see page 66).

Saint Arnold – the patron saint of brewers – yes really! Arnold was born in Belgium in 1040, and was Sir Arnold of Stella before he took holy waters. He thoughtfully encouraged the locals to drink beer instead of water – top man. (This was allegedly because beer was free of nasty bugs and therefore safer, but we know the truth.) Saint Arnold's day is celebrated on 18 August, which every self-respecting beer drinker should petition to be a national holiday. Cheers, holy big ears!

Clint Eastwood – gunslinging cowboy, film director, actor, apparently loves his Newcastle Brown … If the Marlboro Man made cigarettes sexy, then Clint makes Newkie Brown fuckin' irresistible.

Finally we're going to include **ourselves** for what we're doing and 'cos we think we're true beer heroes.

To be a true beer hero you need to be familiar with a special kind of language. Beer and drinking has its own particular jargon, which we're happy to share with you (see next page). Drop these words into pub talk and see what happens – there will be lots of different ideas and variations, which you should talk about and expand on. Create your own local beer dialect, have your own local lingo.

MORRISSEY MAXIM
*Not buying a round is like
not wanting to have friends.*

Drinktionary

Alement *noun.* Any condition, including hangover, injury to self and others, destruction of property, caused by excessive beer consumption. *'I'm not coming in to work today – I picked up an **alement** last night.'*

Beermentor *noun.* Person, usually adult, who led one to underage drinking and educated the unformed drinking palate. *'Nobby Shingles wasn't just my PE teacher, he was my **beermentor** – used to get me pissed.'*

Beer Pump *noun.* Full erection caused by beer-induced lust. *'She may be fugly but I couldn't help myself. After 14 pints it was all hands to the **beer pump**.'*

Beer Zero *noun.* A period of time demarcated as alcohol free by an authority greater than yourself, e.g. *'Are you coming to the pub tonight?'* *'No, my girlfriend has declared this evening a **beer zero**, as we have to go shopping for curtains tomorrow.'*

Beyond the pale *phrase.* Reaching for **The Top Shelf**.

Bitterness *noun.* State of ill feeling to fellow man, brought on by over-consumption of Real Ale.

Bottom fermenting *verb.* Preparing beer farts.

Brewers' Stoop *noun.* A semi-erection caused by overdrinking.

Changing lanes *verb.* Moving from one type of alcoholic beverage to another in order to increase or decrease level of inebriation. *'It's half past nine and I'm still in the land that time forgot. I'm going on the Inside Lane for a bit.'* **Sitting in the middle lane** is slang for a pint and chaser combination.

Chasing the peanut *verb.* Eating salty snacks in order to build thirst for next pint.

Chimps Fingers (*pl* **Chingers**) *noun.* Dark, malty bullet-shaped poo induced by Guinness bender.

Cider Vision *noun.* Finding members of the opposite sex, same sex, animals and other objects infinitely more attractive under influence of cider or scrumpy. Someone deliberately intoxicated by another with apple beverage has been **blind cidered**. Usually young person.

Cider stalking *verb.* Six pints of scrumpy and you think that the lovely lady at the bar has eyes only for you. When she leaves you casually walk out after her only to bump into her huge boyfriend …

Flooring the beer pedal *verb.* The act of getting a sneaky pint in before it's decided who is to stay in **the land that time forgot.**

Fostering *verb.* Going for cheap, chemical shit beer in the mistaken belief that it will do you less harm (also **Carling**).

Gandhishandy *noun.* Lager and lemonade drink available to the designated driver in a party at an Indian restaurant.

Handyshandy *noun.* The one-stop diluted beer favoured by drivers who are quickly moving on.

Hopping about *verb.* Jigging on the spot to forestall **Keg Island** or **Trouser Tsunami.**

Keg Island *noun.* Small stain patch in crotch of trousers – often precursor to **Trouser Tsunami.**

The Land That Time Forgot *noun.* Often-enforced state of being sober in heavy drinking environment for prolonged period (i.e. longer than ten minutes).

Mash tun *verb.* Drinking way more than you should with reckless

abandon. '*Last Friday I was **mash tun** on the Top Shelf. It was messy.*'

Mother Superior *noun.* Woman who lets everybody in the pub know that she's only having one because she is a responsible parent (also **Homo Superior** – man).

Original Gravity *noun.* State of being before serious beer consumption gets underway.

Pork Scratchings *noun.* Repulsive member of the opposite sex rendered irresistible by drink.

Top Shelf *noun.* The place where spirits are kept. The highest rung on the bar. A place to be visited with extreme caution, especially if you are **mash tun.**

Trouser Tsunami *noun.* Total urinary incontinence, brought on by **mash tun.**

Twat of Nine Ales *noun.* One who makes fool of himself on dance floor after drinking too much, in order to procure some **pork scratchings.**

Welsh Rabbit *verb.* One who talks profound bullshit after three pints.

Yeaster Sunday *noun.* Farting caused by beer and heavy roast lunch combination.

Drinking games

Apart from inventing your own lingo, another traditional way of relaxing in your local is to play a traditional drinking game ...

Celebrity Slosh

A 'vicious circle' game, where losing once greatly increases your chances of losing again, as a degree of quick thinking is required. A player starts by saying the name of someone famous – Celebrity A. The next person must say a name (Celebrity B) that starts with the first letter of the last name of Celebrity A. And so on. So: David Bowie – Brad Pitt – Penny Lancaster – Lionel Ritchie etc.

If a player can't think of an appropriate name immediately, they must drink for the duration until they can. Play never stops, but if someone says a celebrity with a single name (e.g. Madonna, Sting), or with first and last names beginning with the same letter, then the direction of play reverses. Guaranteed to produce drunken arguments about celebrity status.

Best after: **ONE PINT**

Beer Hunter

The rules are so easy a drunk person could understand them. All you need for this game is a six-pack, a box and people. Take one can and shake it. Really shake it. Now shake it again. Put it in the box with the other cans, making sure that one person isn't looking as you do this. Get that person to mix the cans around now, so no one should know which is your 'full chamber' beer. The first to go picks a can, holds it to their head at an angle and pulls the tab. If it's not the primed can, they have to drink it, and the next person goes. If it is, they get a wet head and you reload the box. In homage to the famous Russian Roulette sequence in *The Deer Hunter*.

Best after: **TEN + PINTS**

Beer Race

Another game for simple drunks. Each player has a full pint. Everyone starts to down their drinks at the same time. When the quickest has finished, they must turn their glass upside down and place it on their head. When this happens, all remaining players must do the same, regardless of what's left in their glass.

Of course, you could make it two or three pints before finishing …
Very, very messy!

Best after: **TEN + PINTS**

Depth Charge

You'll need a jug of beer, a half-pint glass and nerves of steel. Float the half-pint glass in the pitcher. In turn, each player pours beer from their glass into the floater. The one who sinks it, drinks a beer. Skills to master include filling the glass just about to the brim, so the next player will inevitably sink it; or releasing just a drop of ale, to counter the previous strategy. Shaking the table is *verboten*.

Best after: **EIGHT PINTS**

Buzz Fuzz

Another 'vicious circle' game. The game starts with someone saying 'one' and continuing clockwise ('two'; 'three', etc.) until you get to a multiple of seven (i.e. 'seven') when you must say 'buzz'. Play switches direction until the next 'buzz' (i.e. '14'). To make things more complicated, on every multiple of five, or a number with five in it, you say 'fuzz' but do not switch direction. If a number has both five and seven in it, you must say 'buzz fuzz'. If a player messes up, they drink up. Play resumes from the mistake and it just gets harder.

Best after: **TWO PINTS**

Go Peanut!

Each player needs a full pint and a peanut, which they drop into their glass at the same time. Once the peanut hits the bottom of the glass, it will slowly rise up to the surface again. The player whose peanut reaches the top last must down the pint. Hint: don't even think about playing this game with pints of *Guinness*.

Best after: **SIX PINTS**

James Bond

Put on a James Bond film – any will do, though we'd recommend the Connery vintage, or a bit of Roger. Agree the measure, then:
>   Every time someone says 'James', drink.
>   Every time someone says 'Bond', drink.
>   Every time someone says 'James Bond', drink twice.
>   Watch out for 'My name is Bond, James Bond'.

Best after: **FIVE PINTS**

Matchbox Disaster

All you need is a box of matches and several players with full pints. Each player takes it in turns to throw the matchbox into the middle of the table. If the box lands on its front or back, the turn passes clockwise to the next player. But if it lands on the long thin side, add two fingers of beer to the count. If it lands on either end of the box, add four fingers. Keep throwing until it lands on a flat side again. The box is then passed on to the next person, who gets one throw. If this player lands the front or back, they have to down the amount of beer in the count. Sit to the left of someone who's rubbish at throwing if you can. You can refine the scoring by adding two fingers if the box falls off the table, and by downing your drink if you throw the matches in it. If you throw the box into another player's glass, down it and get them a new one!

Best after: **THREE PINTS**

Fuzzy Duck

The game starts off by someone saying 'fuzzy duck' to the person to their left. This process continues around the table until someone says 'does he?' The direction reverses but now players have to say 'ducky fuzz' instead. This carries on until someone says 'does he?' again, when players must revert to 'fuzzy duck'. This game needs to be played fast. When someone gets the words wrong they must down their drink. If somebody says 'does he?' twice in a row, they must also down the drink, dirty cheats!

Best after: **TWO PINTS**

MORRISSEY MAXIM

Drink equal measures to your date; if she drinks more than you, don't go anywhere near her.

Beer

Drinking

The Pub

Food

Morrissey and Foxy's almost entirely serious history of the pub

Pubs. Where would beer be without them? For as long as they've existed in their many forms, people have been saying that they weren't like that in my day, and that they don't know what will become of them. And they're certainly changing now, with sports pubs, gastropubs and theme pubs replacing the typical city centre boozer, but also the country pub holding its own and quality beers making a comeback at the pump. Presenting Morrissey and Foxy's almost entirely serious history of the pub – a short canter through British hostelry history.

M: So, Foxy, did you know that the Romans invented the pub?

> **F:** Yes, Neil, I did. They set up taverns for troops to quench their thirst in between bouts of fighting the natives – a tradition which lingers on today with the Squaddie pub. Incidentally, the taverns were marked with bunches of vine leaves, which were the first example of the pub signs we know and love.

M: Fascinating. Of course, when the Romans left, it was the alewives who took over brewing, making beer alongside bread for the whole community to enjoy. Alehouses became established. And the bigger, more popular ones became known as 'public houses'. Voilà – a forerunner of the modern-day drinking den.

> **F:** Yes, but around the same time another type of pub emerged and, like the Roman taverns, this one was related to travel.

M: Really?

F: Yes, pilgrimages, like the ones Chaucer wrote about in *The Canterbury Tales*, were incredibly popular in days of yore. And, in the 12th century, commercial travel between towns was on the increase. Of course, all these travellers needed somewhere to stay and something to eat and drink. While the monasteries had provided these services, and indeed brewed their own beer, the surge in demand led to the creation of roadside inns, a sort of medieval Travelodge. Unlike the modern day Travelodge, these inns eventually offered lavish hospitality and were considered safe places to stay – a refuge from the highwaymen who plagued our country lanes.

M: And I bet a plate of chips didn't cost ten quid. Interesting. In the towns, taverns flourished in Elizabethan times, as gentlemen gathered to drink imported wine and, of course, beer. Coffee and tea also became widely available, though sadly onion rings were still a thing of the future for your Shakespeare-loving quaffer. Imagine being desperate for a piss in a pair of tights.

F: Of course your taverns looked like the dogs nadgers alongside the gin shops that sprang up in the 17th century, when the government of the day had a Top Shelf moment and made spirits cheaper than beer. Gin, or some 180 per cent proof brainsplat of destruction called gin, became the city dweller's beverage of choice, which is why your gentlemen graduated to taverns, and beer became respectable.

M: About time. And look at our pubs today – alcopops, what the fuck's that all about? Anyway, in the 18th and 19th centuries, taverns became even more respectable – to distinguish themselves from drinking dens. Ornate furnishing and grand interior design like pillars and plaster decorations became the flavour of the day. Then the Victorians arrived. Uptight little buggers, the Victorians.

F: Yes. The Temperance Movement took off and set about persuading the working classes to 'sign the Pledge' and give up drinking for the good of their souls and their families. And for the factories the middle-class businessmen, with their twirly moustaches, wanted them to work in. This trend continued in the early 20th century, with legislation being brought in to curb the opening hours of the pub, as it had finally become known. This was done in the First World War, so we could produce more weapons, but amazingly survived into this century.

M: And here we are. No world wars, no tights, no dandy highwaymen and not much sign of monks. Now your typical pub is likely to be part of a chain, stuck between *Greggs the Bakers* and *Boots* in the high street, offering karaoke and quiz nights in place of conversation and bonhomie. Fight nights on Fridays and Saturdays. The corporates have taken over, mate, peddling their chemical piss to punters too busy watching *Sky Sports* to notice. No wonder pubs are closing at the rate of 60 a week. This is not the future. Gawd blimey, pass me that gin …

F: But pubs will change and survive. They always have. They've withstood the Romans, gin, the Victorians, the Hofmeister. Feisty little buggers, aren't they? Phew! Fancy a pint?

M: Cheers!

Pub culture

We've looked through frothy spectacles at the essential ingredient in any pub – the beer. And now our bleary gaze comes to rest on the drinkers. Respecting beer is certainly one essential for any modern drinker; respecting the rules of the pub follows a close second in our view. The pub is one of our greatest institutions and should be treated like the treasure it is. So, here is a short guide to good pub behaviour.

The dos and don'ts of the pub

1. Do get your round in

What could be simpler? You're there with your mates, you take it in turns. But some recent examples of the Bar Swerve prompt this. Don't know what the Bar Swerve is? Read on.

The Bar Swerve – how not to get your round in

Some people go to extremes not to peel open the wallet; they think it's some sort of honorary thing to come out of the pub with more money than they went in with. No. Can't do that. Watch out for the following tell-tale signs:

i) The mate who goes to the loo just before it's his round (otherwise known as 'timing your toilet').

ii) The mate who insists (usually at the end of a long night), 'I got the last one'. Yeah, right.

iii) The mate at the end of a long night who says, 'I've had enough now' and heads off home.

iv) The urgent phone call outside which takes ten minutes, by which time someone has got the next one in.

2. Don't jump the queue at the bar

Should be a no-brainer this one but, in the Vomitoriums on the High Street, it's a free-for-all at the bar. This must not happen in a pub. Just as you know your place in the queue at the barbers, so knowing your place at the bar is an essential part of pub etiquette. Don't be tempted by the free market, Darwinian idea of getting your pint ahead of someone smaller, less thrusting or insistent than you – wait your turn. Good things come to those who do so …

3. Don't embark on explicit sexual journeys in the middle of a crowded pub

Most of us don't mind watching a bit, but if you or your new love decide that the rammed pub on 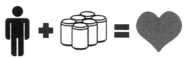 a Friday night is a good place, think again. Take her outside. Otherwise, you will always be caught and most likely BE BARRED. Your budding relationship might not survive that trauma.

4. Don't drink a yard of ale if you've got a cold

You'll die.

While we're talking of things not to do, here's a quick list of things that are completely wrong in a pub:

Smooth flow. A crap idea at the time, and it hasn't improved with age.
Extra Cold. It's no coincidence that the more you chill something the less it tastes of anything. It doesn't take Einstein to figure out what's going on here.
Anything blue (apart perhaps from Curacao). Just because it's got a bright colour and gets you off your tits in no seconds flat doesn't mean it's a good drink.
Horse brasses. Why?

Right, rant over. Let's get back to the good stuff.

Meet the regulars

A pub – a good pub – should be the centre of any community, and will attract people from all walks of life – wobbly old folk, underage drinkers, red-faced snorters. A pub is a great equaliser and no one is better than anyone else once they walk over that threshold. Below is Morrissey and Foxy's guide to The Regulars.

You walk into the classic English country pub. Low oak beams frame a classic bar where real ale pumps stand to attention in front of you begging to be pulled. This is the place people come when they want to understand the essence of 'pub' – what makes the pub the focus of the community. There are regulars in the pub gathered around the bar clearly entirely comfortable in their surroundings – perhaps more at home than when they are at home. They come in many shapes and sizes but there are definitely 'types'.

The Moaner – the man is a miracle. Nothing has any effect on his miserable outlook. If he won the Lottery he'd complain about all those thieving charities begging for a wodge; if the sun is shining, he'd moan about the inevitability of a hosepipe ban; if any cloud has a silver lining, he thinks it's lead. Nothing but nothing will make him crack a smile, unless, of course, something particularly bad has just happened to his family or friends.

The Waterfront – his life is spent checking the rearview mirror. Once, just once, thirty years ago, he nearly did something that would have changed the course of his life. But it didn't happen – a fact that he never tires of telling anyone who will listen. He could have been the next James Dean, Tom Jones's pants maker, the Queen's Corgi Brusher or President of the United States of America, if he just hadn't had this one piece of bad luck.

The Trivia King – a man so steeped in useless knowledge he can produce a statistic on any subject you care to throw at him: frogs, hangover cures, Liberal Democrats, tin cans or the Vietnam War. *The Guinness Book of Records* is his bedtime reading; Fred Dineage is his idol and he once made it to the qualifying heats of *Mastermind*. Inevitably he gets Nietzsche into the fucking conversation at some stage too – always bloody Nietzsche. This man has no opinions of his own – merely tedious, useless knowledge. Very useful for the crossword, though.

The 1275th in Line for the Throne – like The Waterfront, there is always someone in the pub who has a distant claim to the English throne. Pointed out by other regulars to the pub novices, the 1275th in Line to the Throne, is treated as everyone else is in the pub to his face but there is a touch of reverence employed when talking about him. It adds a shade of regal purple to all regulars in the pub. Distant Throne Man (as he is also called) is aware that he is lauded but feigns – big word – insouciance as befits his regal bearing,

The Spiv – always has a tip about a good piece of business to be done. Could be some shares trading at a low price which 'he has on good authority from a person who should know' (wink) that will see a sudden 'upturn' in value. Could be a nice piece of lead coming his way, which he needs to offload sharpish. He has all the financial vocabulary off pat and always knows the right people. If you have something to offer in return, he will look as if he's listening, then completely ignore the advice – he's the only one with the knowledge. Sadly, he doesn't seem to profit much from the inside track as he's always broke.

The Colonel – saw action in the Second World War – 'a crack at the hun' – and has the ruddy nose to prove that the trauma drove him directly to drink and he hasn't come back yet. Frequently reaches for the Top Shelf and doesn't care about the quality or type of the stuff that comes from there. Alcohol By Volume is what he's after and he has to have a certain amount every session. Manages to keep a straight back throughout, though.

The Pub Bore – a mix of the Trivia King and the annoying bloke at school who always tagged along and no one had the heart to tell him to 'fuck off'. The Pub Bore is tolerated because no degree of insult will dent his sunny good humour. If you want to vent spleen there is no better butt to aim at than the Pub Bore. When not being abused by regulars he collars unsuspecting visitors, fixes them with his unflinching eyes and talks and talks and talks. And then, when the visitor thinks he has stopped and is preparing the exit line, he starts again. He has a different fact every day to kick off the conversation.

The Village Historian – like the 1275th in Line to the Throne, the Village Historian is spoken of with a touch more reverence to out-of-towners than the other regulars. Ask a question of the landlord in this village pub about when such and such a building was put up, you will invariably get the answer 'Ask George – he was here when the Ark floated by'. Also, inevitably, you're not allowed to ask George, because the landlord will then shout across to him (thereby showing how easily he chats to this pillar of the community), ''Ere, George, gentleman here wants to know when Dick Turpin rode through the village. Said you were probably there!'

The Odd Couple – are not odd at all, which is what makes them stand out. Octogenarian loafers, who come in of a lunchtime for a single drink – him half a bitter, her a schooner of sherry. They nurse their tipples well into the evening while sitting perfectly still and staring directly ahead, as if communing with Buddha. Might exclaim, 'Well, didn't it turn out nice?' or 'There was a Chinese man in the village last week', but don't really go for conversation, as such. After 61 years of marriage, there is nothing fate can throw to unbalance them. Highly likely to murder each other one morning over an argument about who didn't put the cat out the night before.

Pub landlords and staff

It's not just the regulars who come in handy to recognise types. From the other side of the bar we present:

The landlords

The Retired Military Type – he runs a tight ship until he opens the pub, at which point the Top Shelf beckons and the ruddy veins in his nose start to throb ... He takes every 'and one for yourself' on offer and, by the end of the night, uses the bar to navigate in a straight line. He promises to go on the 'straight and narrow' but always tomorrow ... until tomorrow's opening time that is.

The Likely Lad – he's everyone's friend – everyone he knows and everyone he has ever met. Familiar to the point of rudeness, he tries too hard to establish an instant rapport and makes you vow never to go back in. The 'regulars' are there because he always gets his round in.

Career Man/Woman – these people studied Catering Management Systems, but they have absolutely no interest in drink or in the public; they spend their whole working life thinking about customer satisfaction questionnaires, the bottom line and how to get and serve as many dregs out of the barrel as possible. The Career Manager (not really a landlord) takes the bar very seriously, so seriously that, at the first outbreak of anyone actually enjoying themselves, he sets the bouncers on them.

The Grumpiest Man Alive – so the pub is somewhere to go and have a good time? Not to this man – a character so terminally grumpy he finds comfort only in making people's lives a misery. If you approach the bar with a smile, his stony, hostile face makes you beat a retreat; the atmosphere in the pub is so subdued you think you've stumbled into a wake; the only regulars are, therefore, depressive masochists.

The Alchie – like The Retired Military Type his sole (or perhaps soul) purpose is to get lathered every day. If he can cash up at the end of the night, he's not had a good day. Red-faced, usually impossibly cheery, but with such a rapid ability to turn nasty you are walking on egg shells all the time. This man's pub is neglected to the point of abandonment.

The Gangster – oh dear. You walk into this one at your peril. Populated by men in shiny suits and others with tattoos in places that are all too visible, with teardrops and spiders' webs to the fore, this pub reeks of danger. The landlord probably has a one-word nickname ('Scissors' is a bit of a giveaway). The conversation is subdued and you engage Scissors in conversation with extreme caution. Don't mention that your cousin works in any form of the law – even if he's an RSPCA inspector. Drink up and get out.

The Ex-footballer – a dying breed, most frequently spotted in the Home Counties. The once-imposing physique has slumped somewhat, but there still remains enough of a clue to his former occupation. He will joke about it, but will invariably be bitter about the massive rewards on offer to your 'very average' Premiership player. The irony is you had to be top of your game to retire to a pub in his day; now you'd have to be Conference shite, and even then you'd become a sports psychologist, 'whatever that is'. Attracts more than his fair share of over-the-hill footballer's totty and is worshipped by the Sunday league team he coaches – the highlight of his week.

The Celebrity's Son – dreamt of owning a restaurant, but couldn't make it until Dad stepped in and fronted the cash. Feels a mixture of joy and resentment. Celebrity Dad paid for the refurb, and hired the talented young chef. And invited his newspaper friends to come and dine in the restaurant with his celebrity friends. But it's all down to the son that it's become a success. No, really.

These characters are national institutions. We should erect plaques to them in all pubs they grace. And, talking of national institutions, here's our guide to pub names: the most popular and how some came about.

Pub names

That other essential – the pub sign – was made compulsory by
Richard II in 1393 because most of the population couldn't read.
Brightly painted signs helped them tell their alehouse from their
cobblers. Pub names evolved in many different ways – the sign
might have reflected a local trade, or an allegiance, or that the
landlord was a creepy guy. Many have stood the Teste of Tyme,
though some have passed into Ye Olde Obscuritie.

Here's some of the weirdest:

The Bucket of Blood, Phillack, Cornwall (landlord went to gather water
from the well and drew blood instead – a body was later discovered at
the foot of the well)

Bull & Spectacles, Staffordshire (renamed when a Top Shelfer climbed
up and placed his specs on the Bull's Head)

The Cat & Custard Pot, Kent (formally called The Cat & Mustard Pot)

Cow & Snuffers, Cardiff

Donkey on Fire, Ramsgate, Kent

The Drunken Duck, Ambleside, Cumbria

The Duke without a Head, Wateringbury, Kent

The Inn Next Door Burnt Down, Bedfordshire

The Jolly Taxpayer, Plymouth (Inland Revenue offices were once
located nearby)

The Leg of Mutton and Cauliflower, Ashtead, Surrey

Labouring Boys, Isleworth, Middlesex

Built in 1667 – the original burned down in the Great Fire – patrons of Ye Olde Cheshire Cheese *have included* Charles Dickens and Sir Arthur Conan Doyle. *One famous resident was a parrot whose mimicry entertained customers for 40 years. Its death was announced on the BBC and obituaries appeared in newspapers.*

The Lion of Vienna, Bolton (named after Bolton Wanderers football legend Nat Lofthouse)

Muscular Arms, Glasgow

Nobody Inn, Dartmoor

The Old Thirteenth Cheshire Astley Volunteer Rifleman Corps Inn, Stalybridge (Longest Pub Name)

Peveril of the Peak, Dovedale, Derbyshire (named after a stagecoach)

Q, Stalybridge (Shortest Pub Name)

The Quiet Woman, York (the sign shows a woman carrying her own severed head)

Round of Carrots, Herefordshire

Spinner & Bergamot, Comberbach, Cheshire

The Strawbury Duck, Entwistle, Lancashire

Twice Brewed Inn, near Haltwhistle, Northumberland (A troop of soldiers stopped for a pint, and when they tasted the beer, decided it wasn't strong enough so it had to be brewed again)

Who'd a Thowt It, Middleton, Manchester

World Turned Upside Down, Old Kent Road, London, SE1

Young Vanish, Chesterfield (named after a racehorse), Derbyshire

Here are a few of the more easily explained:

Red Lion – This became the most popular inn name when James VI of Scotland inherited the throne of England and joined the rampant lion of Scotland with the three leopards of England. The King 'suggested' that the red lion sign be displayed as a mark of respect. Innkeepers everywhere shat themselves and rushed out to buy some red paint.

Rose & Crown – Some innkeepers had bigger cojones. Any pub with a Crown in its name represented a sign of loyalty to the monarch. The Rose is England's flower, and The Rose & Crown appeared as a pub name not long after James VI was 'encouraging' Red Lions all over the place. It was a way for English landlords to say, 'You're the Man, but we're still the English.'

Cock and Bull – The story goes that the customers of neighbouring pubs in Buckinghamshire, called The Cock and The Bull, were great rivals and well-versed in 'the joy of talking shit' (see page 107). The stories they told of their achievements, which were total bollocks, became known as 'cock and bull stories' and, for obvious reasons, this became a popular pub name.

Crown & Anchor – Retired naval officers who set up pubs often used the name to show their loyalty to the monarch and the navy. The Lord High Admiral had the Crown & Anchor on his coat of arms. It was also a reminder of a time when 'three sheets to the wind' meant something else entirely.

White Hart – See Red Lion. The White Hart was on Richard II's coat of arms and he was a right bastard at the best of times.

Swan With Two Necks – The Worshipful Company of Vintners were granted the right to own swans by Elizabeth I – after she'd had a few brews one morning, no doubt. To distinguish their swans, they marked the beaks with two nicks, or 'necks', and there you have it. The Vintners still participate in the annual ceremony of 'swan upping' on the Thames. It's a privilege, apparently.

Marquis of Granby – Great beater of the French at war, the Marquis was also prone to giving his loyal officers a pub when they retired. Like footballers in the 1970s. As a mark of gratitude, they would name the pub after him.

Pig & Whistle – The phrase 'Pigs and Whistles' dates back more than 300 years, and means 'Rack and ruin'. Need we say more?

Fawcett Inn – Not all pubs are named after famous people. This one recalls that unhappy situation you sometimes encounter when you get jiggy after a lot of ale. Train ticket in a parking meter, anyone?

Right, these are the most common names in use today. Show me a town that doesn't have one of these, or more likely all of them, in it.

1. **Red Lion**
2. **Crown**
3. **Royal Oak**
4. **Swan**
5. **White Hart**
6. **Bell**
7. **Plough**
8. **King's Head**
9. **Railway**
10. **New Inn**
11. **Ship**
12. **White Horse**
13. **George**
14. **King's Arms**
15. **Rose and Crown**
16. **Wheatsheaf**
17. **Queen's Head**
18. **Black Horse**
19. **Prince of Wales**
20. **Victoria**

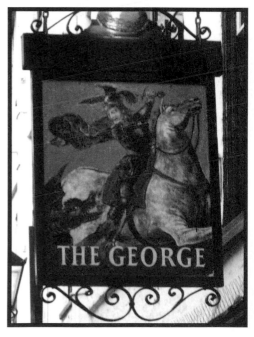

A crawl around some fictional pubs

The pub's importance to British culture (hic) is well shown by its prominence in some of our best-loved films and TV programmes. Here is but half-a-pint's worth of our favourites.

The Prancing Pony in *The Lord of the Rings*

At the sign of the Prancing Pony, where Frodo meets Strider, or Aragorn, for the first time. Frodo draws attention to himself by falling and accidentally slipping on his ring. Not an easy manoeuvre but probably easier after a fat bowl of pipe weed and a skinful of Barliman Butterbur's ale. Of the things not to do while drunk, one of the top is probably go off into the wilderness with a man in a cape and a very long shiny sword ...

Best beer not served: **Black Rider** (stout – cold, dark and best avoided)

The Winchester in *Shaun of the Dead*

Most of this wickedly funny zombie film is set in or around the Winchester public house – second home to Shaun and Ed and, less appreciatively, Shaun's ex-girlfriend Liz. The climax of the film sees them holed up in the pub surrounded by marauding flesh-eaters, with Shaun demonstrating Yoda-level 'beer talk':

SHAUN: 'As Bertrand Russell once said, "The only thing that will redeem mankind is cooperation." I think we can all appreciate the relevance of that now.'

LIZ: 'Was that on a beer mat?'

SHAUN: 'Yeah, it was *Guinness Extra Cold*.'

LIZ: 'I won't say anything.'

SHAUN: 'Thanks.'

Best beer not served: **Living Dead** (lager – leaves you feeling like death warmed up)

The Rovers Return in *Coronation Street*

Mother and father of all fictional pubs, with its own fictional brewery – Newton and Ridley – to boot. It even has a fictional history going way back to 1902, when Coronation Street was built to mark the coronation of Edward VII. Since then it has been the site of many of the street's top stories including the lorry crash of 1979 and the fire of 1986. It's been a free house since 1996, and serves brews from Nuttall's Ales alongside Newton and Ridley's. The pub was revamped in 2008 to bring it up to date. Piss-cheap lager replaced the ales, they put *Sky TV* in and hired a bouncer to clear up the drug dealing. Pint of Pledge Buster anyone?

Best beer not served: **Duckworth's Blonde** (have you talking nonsense after a pint)

The Queen Vic in *EastEnders*

TV's second most famous pub also has a long fictional history, according to which it used to be called the Balmoral. The name was changed as a tribute to Prince Albert following his death. In its 20-odd year history, the pub has witnessed death, rape, murder, and arson. Oh, and a wedding. Full of slags, geezers and variety entertainers on the lookout for a second lucrative career.

Best beer not served: **Dirty Den** (disappears easily but comes back with a vengeance)

The Nag's Head in *Only Fools and Horses*

The Nag's Head is Peckham's finest, favourite watering hole, where the 'joys of talking shit', 'beer talk', and 'The Bar Swerve' are to be seen at their best. Landlord Mike keeps an iron grip on proceedings, and Trigger provides unintentional pearls of wisdom:

MIKE: 'Don't try 'n' be funny with me, Trigger. I'll tell you this much, I've had certificates for my beer.'
TRIGGER: 'Yeah, I've had a few days off work with it as well!'

Best beer not served: **Trotters' Independent Ale** (comes with a free Russian ex-army handheld camcorder)

Traditional pub games

Nowadays, when you walk into a pub, you'll very likely hear the repetitive jingle of a fruit machine or trivia game – games in pubs, aside from quizzes, have become a solitary activity, a way of getting away from your other half, and, to be honest, a bit of a bore.

Games used to be more part of a community and many of them were as mad as a box of frogs – rhubarb thrashing, anyone? Thankfully, there are still many parts of the UK where traditional pub games, dating back hundreds and sometimes thousands of years, still flourish. Indeed there are signs that some old favourites, nutty though they seem, are making a comeback. Bring on the sound of dwile on girter, the clink of quoit on hob. Here's our guide to some of the best and weirdest games around.

Bar Billiards
Great game, which came to our pubs in the 30s after an Englishman named David Gill spotted it in Belgium where it was called 'Russian Bar Billiards'. Why Russian, we don't know. Bar billiards is like billiards except the 'pockets' are holes on the table, some of which are guarded by skittles, which must not be knocked over, except right at the end, or something like that. The tables are just beautiful and take up less valuable pub space than billiard tables. Awesome game still played in leagues around the UK, though pool has done for it in many places.

Shovel Board and Shove Ha'penny
The mother of all English 'shoving' games, including Shove Ha'penny, Shovel Board was originally played in Tudor times on narrow tables as long as 9 metres. The idea was to shove metal weights as near to the end of the table without them falling off. It's thought that this began as an upper class pastime played on tables after dinner, probably with peasants instead of weights. King Henry VIII used to gamble on Shovel Board

while banning his subjects from playing it. Probably where the expression 'You can Shove it' came from!

Shove Ha'penny came about in the 15th century as a smaller version that could be played in taverns. In the game, players push or 'shove' coins up a board with horizontal lines across it. The areas between each pair of horizontal lines are called 'beds' and, to win, a player needs to get a coin in each of the beds three times without touching the lines – not easy! Shoving techniques include using the heel of the hand, the palm and the side of the thumb. The game is still played in many pubs.

Quoits

For hundreds of years people have thrown metal rings up and down a pitch at stakes, or 'hobs'. There are many variants on what became 'quoits' and some great vocabulary to match. Official rules first appeared in an 1881 edition of *The Field*, having been decided on by a group of Northern England pubs. The 'Bibber' or 'Shower up' stands by the stake and shouts advice, which might come in handy if you get a 'front toucher', 'side toucher' or 'back toucher'.

Ringing the Bull

The aim is to swing a metal ring, attached to the ceiling by a rope, onto a bull's horn on the wall. Nowadays a metal hook is often used. This is one of the oldest of all pub games, and legend has it that it was brought back from Jerusalem by the Crusaders in the 12th century. Well that's what they say at The Trip to Jerusalem pub in Nottingham, where they still hold an annual 'Ringing the Bull' contest! The ultimate challenge is to circle the room twice before landing the ring. Watch out for passing punters.

Toad in the Hole

Brass discs – 'toads' – are thrown at a hole in a table about eight feet away. Each player gets four toads per turn, with two points for a 'toad in the hole' and one point for a toad on the table. Toad in the hole is likely to be a version of the European 'Frog', but no one really seems to know for sure. An international 'Toad in the Hole' competition is held in Sussex – the 2006 fixture attracted 192 competitors in 48 teams!

Dwile Flonking

Definite Top Shelf material this one. The game is officially played by two teams of twelve players. The fielding team gathers in a 'girter', or circle, surrounding the other team's 'flonker'. The flonker holds the 'driveller' – a broom handle topped by a beer-soaked rag, or 'dwile'. The girter then dances around the flonker in a circle. He must flick (or flonk) the dwile with the driveller so it hits a girter team member. His score depends on which part of the body he hits. The usual scoring is three points for a hit on the head (a *wanton*), two for a hit on the body, (a *marther*), and just one for a leg strike (a *ripple*). If, after two shots, the flonker hasn't scored, he is *swadged*, or *potted*, which means he has to drink a quantity of beer from a chamber pot within a given time. After all the members of one team have flonked, the other team is put in. The winner is the team with the most points after two innings, usually the one with more members still upright. Mental as anything.

Conger cuddling

The most fun you can have with a dead fish? One team of nine stands on six-inch high wooden blocks and the other teams take it in turn to swing a 11.3kg eel, attached to a rope, at them. The winning team is the one with the most men standing after each contestant has had a swing.

This fishy game was banned in 2006, when animal rights activists claimed it was 'disrespectful' to the dead eel. Previously it had been staged annually for more than 30 years in Lyme Regis, Dorset, to raise funds for the Royal National Lifeboat Institution. There is talk of using a plastic fish! Retired publican Richard Fox organised the first contest in the 1970s!

Rhubarb thrashing

All you need to 'thrash the rhubarb' is a couple of dustbins (wheelies will do), blindfolds and a good supply of rhubarb. Oh, and a couple of idiots. The blindfolded idiots stand in the bins, facing each other, and then hit each other round the head with the rhubarb sticks until one gives in. Simple, and a great spectator sport! No idea where this came from, but definitely due a comeback. Another one for lovers of the Top Shelf.

Pub jokes

When all is said and done, laughter is the sound most often heard in pubs. Convivial chat, a chance to let your hair down after a hard slog at work, meeting up with mates for a night out – all these situations demand a bit of a laugh. And where would pub laughter be without pub jokes? Here is an offering of Morrissey and Foxy's favourite 'man walks into a pub' style gags ...

A man walks into a bar with a steering wheel in his underpants.

'Is that painful?' the barman asks.

'It's driving me nuts!' the man replies.

> A woman walked into a bar carrying a duck under her arm.
>
> 'Get that pig out of here!' yelled the bartender.
>
> 'That's not a pig, stupid!' she replied. 'That's a duck!'
>
> 'I know!' said the bartender. 'I was talking to the duck!'

A man is sitting in the pub when he hears a bowl of peanuts on the bar saying, 'Oooh, you really are amazing. Oooh, you are lovely.'

Then the fruit machine shouts, 'Rubbish, look at the state of that haircut. And those socks don't go with those shoes.'

The barman apologises. 'I'm sorry,' he says, 'The nuts are complimentary but the fruit machine is out of order.'

> A priest meets a drunk outside a bar. The drunk claims to be Jesus. The priest disagrees, the man insists. Finally, the priest says, 'How can you prove it?' The man says, 'Come with me.' They go inside the bar. The bartender says, 'Jesus Christ, not you again.'

A woman walked into a bar and asked the barman for a double entendre – so he gave her one.

A neutron goes into a bar and asks the barman, 'How much for a beer?'

'For you, no charge,' the barman replies.

An Englishman, an Irishman and a Scotsman walk into a bar and each orders a pint of beer. When the drinks arrive they notice that all three pints have a fly in them. The Englishman looks at his pint in disgust and pushes it away. The Irishman picks out the fly with his fingers, throws it on the floor and proceeds to drink his beer. The Scotsman picks the fly out of his pint, and holds it over the drink shouting, 'Come on you little git, spit it out!'

A man walked into a pub after a long day at work, ordered a pint of beer, and sat down by the bar to enjoy it. Before long he'd finished about half his drink and needed to go to the toilet, so off he went.

While he was away an athletic woman standing in the corner walked up to the bar, picked up the drink, farted into his pint, replaced it, and walked away again.

When the man came back, he sat down to enjoy his pint again, but after he'd taken a mouthful he spat it out and yelled at the barman, 'Oi, barman, this pint tastes disgusting! What's happened to it?'

'Well, you see that woman over there? She farted into it.'

'What?'

'She farted into it. I didn't want to say anything – she looks like she could easily knock seven shades of shit out of me – but that's what she did.'

'Right,' said the bloke, stressed after a long day, 'if you won't say anything, I will.' He got up, went to the woman, and tapped her on her shoulder. She slowly turned around.

'Yes?'

'Er, did you fart in my Whitbread?'

'No, I'm Tessa Sanderson.'

Motorway goes into a pub.

Motorway: 'Give me a pint!'

Barman: 'There you go. That'll be £2.20.'

Motorway: 'I'm not paying for this. I'm mad I am, MAD.'

Barman: 'Alright, alright keep your money.'

Motorway sits in the corner of the pub, drinking its pint.

Dual carriageway goes into the pub.

Dual carriageway: 'Give me a pint!'

Barman: 'There you go. That'll be £2.20.'

Dual carriageway: 'I'm not paying for this. I'm mad I am, MAD.'

Barman: 'Not another nutter.'

Dual carriageway: 'I'm bloody mad, I am.'

Barman: 'Alright, alright keep it.'

Dual carriageway and Motorway sit in the corner of the pub drinking their pints.

Tarmac walks into the pub.

Tarmac: 'Give me a pint.'

Barman: 'There you go. That'll be £2.20.'

Tarmac: 'I'm not paying for this. I'm mad I am, MAD.'

Barman: 'Look I'm not having this. No more free pints!'

Dual carriageway and Motorway (shaking their heads): 'You'd better let him have it, he's a cycle path.'

A plate of Bacon and Eggs walks into a pub. The barman says, 'Sorry, we don't serve breakfast.'

A man walks into a bar with a slab of asphalt under his arm and says, 'A beer please, and one for the road.'

Black Beard the infamous pirate and his crew came to port. They went on shore leave in a bar near the docks. While he was serving drinks, the barman got talking to the pirate.

'Where'd you get that peg leg from?'

'Well, Oi was thrown from me ship during gale force winds, and before me mate could throw me a line, this big ol' shark came along and bit me leg clean orf. Har.'

Later the barman asked, 'And where'd you get that hook, then?'

'Ah, me crew and I were fighting our way through to the treasury and me arm got cut through the bone in a sword fight with the Captain of the Guard.'

Then the barman asked, 'And where'd you get the eye patch from?'

'Har,' the pirate said, 'I was out on deck one day and a gull flew over and crapped in me eye.'

The barman was puzzled. 'How would a gull crapping in your eye make you wear an eye patch?'

'First day with the hook, har har.'

A priest, a nun, a doctor, and a blonde walk into a pub.
The barman says, 'Hey, what is this? Some kind of a joke?'

A man walks into a pub with a giraffe on a lead. 'I'll have a pint of Guinness' says the man, 'and ten pints for the giraffe'. The man then starts to down his pint in one go. The giraffe, seeing this, starts banging down the ten pints like there was no tomorrow. The race is on! The man gets half way down and the giraffe's only on number four. Then, with an amazing burst of speed, the giraffe just manages to scrape ahead. But on pint number ten the giraffe gets halfway, then falls off the bar stool, and passes out on the floor. The man promptly finishes his pint and starts to leave. 'Hey,' says the barman 'you can't leave that lyin' there!' Says the man: 'It's not a lion, it's a giraffe.'

The pub quiz

Pub quizzes have been around for what feels like forever. They most likely came about to compete with TV quizzes, which were keeping punters away from the local. And then, when videos appeared in the 1980s, landlords were even more desperate to get people out of their homes and into the pub.

They're horrible. They attract people who wouldn't normally dream of going to the pub, and don't know how to behave. They form themselves into teams with hilarious names like 'Tears for Beers', or 'Gin'll Fix It'.

Nerdy little men who creep out to the bogs to text their mates, 'Wot is prime root of 75.87? Cheers Nigel'. Or listen in on the next table, who are trying to keep Dawn quiet because she's had two alcopops and gets VERY EXCITED WHEN SHE KNOWS THE ANSWER. Every team contains one self-styled 'genius', who knows the answer to every trivia question ever printed in a trivia book and cannot believe his luck that evolution has finally provided the stage for him to shine on. He bathes in the adoration of his needy teammates, until he is eclipsed one time too many by another tosser.

Quizzes stop people chatting and take over the whole pub, whether you want to take part or not. There's even been a court case caused by a team cheating. How sad is that?

Anyway, for those feeling the need, here is Morrissey and Foxy's very own pub quiz challenge:

1. **In what town did Roy of the Rovers play football?**
2. Why would you be given a green jacket and a yellow jersey?
3. **The berries of what shrub-like plant are used to make gin?**
4. What's the name of the Queen's first Corgi?
5. **What was the official name of the original World Cup?**
6. What did Oscar Wilde consider to be the curse of the drinking classes?
7. **If it's heavy in Scotland, what is it in England?**
8. A granny, a sheepshank and a bowline are all parts of a chimney; true or false?
9. **What are the chances of throwing a double six with two dice?**
10. How much money would you gamble if you bet a brace of ponies?
11. **Where would an American put a weenie?**
12. Who is older, Superman or Batman?
13. **In which sport would you encounter a jerk?**
14. Which drink is produced in the Spanish town of Jerez?
15. **What writer collapsed and died while mixing a mayonnaise?**
16. What guerrilla fighter has a biscuit named after him?
17. **What made Milwaukee famous?**
18. What's the minimum age for a malt whisky?
19. **In what decade did sliced bread first appear?**
20. Which Prime Minster's last words were 'I think I could eat one of Bellamy's veal pies.'?
21. **What food did the Aztecs use as currency?**
22. How many pints of beer are there in a Hogshead?
23. **What region of France does Claret come from?**

24. Where did chocolate originate?

25. **What did the Aztecs cut off what they called the testicle tree?**

26. If herbs are the green part of a plant, what are spices?

27. **What kind of fruit are Green William?**

28. What is dried in an oast?

29. **What was the name of the dog in the children's TV series *The Herbs*?**

30. Who has scored the most goals for England?

31. **What is the name of the pub in Coronation Street?**

32. What's the name of the pub in Emmerdale?

33. **Which song released in 1978 was John Peel's favourite and was played at the DJ's funeral?**

34. Which cocktail is a mixture of champagne and Guinness?

35. **'If you can't beat em, join em' was a successful advertising slogan for which brand of beer?**

36. Australians wouldn't give a 4X for anything other than what?

37. **In cockney rhyming slang, what's happening if you're getting the Britney Spears?**

38. What is the English equivalent of the German 'Rathaus'?
    a) beer cellar
    b) town hall
    c) sewer

39. **In the Simpsons, what is the brand of beer brewed in Springfield?**

40. If you bought a firkin of beer how much would you have? Six pints, two-and-a-half gallons, nine gallons?

41. **How many fluid ounces are there in a pint?**

42. What is Bob the Builder's cat called?

43. **What subject does Neil Morrissey's character, Eddie Lawson teach in Waterloo Road?**

44. What is the food colour cochineal made from?

45. **Which football team is nicknamed the Hornets?**

46. Which TV cook is chairman of Norwich City football club?

47. Who won the first ever World Cup match?

48. Name one of the first South American countries where potatoes were first cultivated.

49. Match the Bond girl to the actress:

1 Xenia Onotopp in *GoldenEye*
2 Solitaire in *Live and Let Die*
3 Mary Goodnight in *The Man with the Golden Gun*
4 Dr Holly Goodhead in *Moonraker*
5 Natalya Simyonova in *Goldeneye*
6 Kara Milovy in *The Living Daylights*
7 Paris Carver in *Tomorrow Never Dies*
8 Honey Rider in *Dr No*
9 Dr Christmas Jones in *The World is Not Enough*
10 May Day in *A View to a Kill*

A Teri Hatcher
B Denise Richards
C Britt Ekland
D Maryan D'Abo
E Grace Jones
F Famke Janssen
G Ursula Andress
H Lois Chiles
I Izabella Scorupco
J Jane Seymour

If you're not a self-styled genius, you can find the answers on page 154.

The joy of talking shit, or why is 'abbreviation' such a long word?

Why do we talk shit in the pub? Because it's the place where we can – we're not allowed at home, certainly not allowed at work. The pub is the only place where you can pontificate to your heart's content and your fellow drinkers nod and understand.

Talking crap in the pub is a release: we love that atmosphere where anything you say is understood, and creating that atmosphere is part of the reason for setting up the pub in the first place. A classic example of this was when we were writing this book. We came up with the theory that the reason so many 70s football players ended up on a bar floor was because they started drinking chemical lager, went to the Top Shelf and crashed mightily to the floor. It's a theory that would get a sage nod from the decent pub companion.

Shit-talk opening gambits

'I've heard …'
'Apparently …'
'A good friend of mine says …'
'I have this on good authority …'

Eight out of ten times the person is talking shit. Check their source. However, this should never lead to doubt or criticism. Talking shit in the pub came shortly after the first sip of beer – they go together like salt and vinegar and alcopops and vomit.

Classic pub talk

A mate of mine who lives in Surrey (and who has this on good authority from a local farmer) says that the foxes near him go round the fences and hawthorn bushes picking off wool from the coats of sheep. They collect a big bundle of wool in their mouth about the size of three tennis balls (remember this is on good authority) and then they go to the nearest pond and, holding the ball of sheep wool in their mouth, reverse into the pond. This is the way they de-flea because, as their body goes into the water, the fleas leap higher and higher up until they find refuge in the wool. Then the fox tosses the wool away, and Bob's your uncle – de-flead.

Great sources of shit talk – used in the pub as often as the one-armed brace – are conspiracy theories. You can rehash the old ones, adding little twists of your own (naturally from 'a good authority') or just reuse the standard ones; whichever approach you take, you're guaranteed an audience and a healthy pint of shit talk. Here is Morrissey and Foxy's Definitive Conspiracy Theory Dossier.

The Apollo Moon Landings were faked in a San Francisco bathroom using cardboard spacecraft, 17 bags of concrete and some cheese.

Diana, Princess of Wales, was murdered by a goat called Simon, riding a moped. He was trained by MI5.

John F. Kennedy was killed by the Seven Dwarves as revenge for the CIA's attempted assassination of Snow White. Well, they've never been caught, have they?

The Premier League is run by ruthless lizards from Outer Space. The day that Middlesborough win the title will be the signal for an alien invasion, and Brian Barwick will reveal himself to be the Supreme Being (there could be something in this one, apparently…).

The world is ruled by four men who meet in the woods every year.

———

Elvis is alive, living with Jim Morrison and Marilyn Monroe
in the Bermuda Triangle.

———

Paul McCartney is actually Jesus reincarnated –
look at the cover of *Abbey Road*, man.

———

While we're on the subject, Jesus was his own sister
and he gave birth to Mary Magdalene.

———

The Titanic was an insurance fraud that went tragically wrong.

———

The New World Order is no longer a conspiracy theory;
it is an established fact. Mankind is now literally entering
a new age, the Age of Aquarius, according to the ancient
zodiacal calendar which is as old as human civilisation.
Aquarius is associated by astrologers with brotherhood,
or fraternity, which is the cornerstone of Freemasonry.
Stick that in your pipe, take it outside and smoke it.

Beer myths

When you're back from the freezing cold lean-to, the next area for discussion is the shit we pretend to know about Beer and Drinking. There are lots of *theories*, some of which are very convenient to the hardened regular. I know they're shit, you know they're shit, we all know they're shit, but we peddle them out anyway.

1. Drink milk before you go out on the raz

Actually, milk is one of the worst things you can drink before an enthusiastic night on the ale. Full of fat, it turns to acid in your stomach and makes you feel awful. Go for lots of carbs, cos salad won't do. (See *Hangover Cures*, page 66).

2. Don't mix the grape and the grain

Complete bollocks. After three bottles of champagne and half a bitter, you wake up with a stinker and say, 'Ah, it was the bitter that did for me; if only I'd stayed on the grape, I'd be fine.' No. It's a myth. You're hungover because you drank too much, or you drank a load of crap. Educate yourself – drink better quality beer and you won't feel so bad.

3. Tequila with a worm that contains peyote

Never has done, never will. It does mean you get to eat some protein while you're knocking back the slammers, though.

4. Drinking a lot kills brain cells

No, it doesn't. This was a myth put about by the bad-tempered Temperance killjoys in the 19th century. It slows down development of new cells apparently so you don't get as brainy as quickly, but, frankly, what would you rather? Faster brain cells or a nice pint? In fact, look at the Research section ...

All of these are said with complete conviction, greeted with silence and then followed up by 'No, seriously... it's true'. The only way to change the conversation is to suggest another round.

Beer talk

Some things are best left unsaid when you've had a few. But they're the things just bursting to come out, after the brew has worked its magic on the restraining bolts. Here's a guide to the things that should and should not be discussed under the influence. As they say in The Slaughtered Lamb, 'Stick to the roads boys, don't stray onto the Moors.'

Good head

Sport – Safe emotional territory which, while promoting friendly banter and rivalry, will not degenerate into mindless violence. Unless you're in Swansea. Or Millwall. Or Portsmouth. But why would you be there?

Machines – See above. You're a bloke. You can argue the pros and cons of a car, TV, mobile or iPod until the end of time. Whose are those feet dangling in front of your face? Oh, your girlfriend's. Who's going to get the next round in now then? Anyway, back to the Audi TT – wanker's car!

Music – Blokes love lists and nothing suits lists like 'best songs of 1988' and 'favourite live performance involving a badger'. Easy way to spot Top Shelf material: 'Oh, I think Bowie just got better and better, though his *Tin Machine* output probably was a creative peak.'

Women – Unless present. Conversation should not stray beyond physical attributes into dark arena of emotions and feelings. That's Women's Talk and best left to them.

Drink – Types of, merits of, strength of, volumes consumed of, whose turn is it to get more of? All good lubricants of the pub conversation chain, and as safe as Top Trumps.

Work – Another great bonder, and flexible. Includes the subheadings: i) My Boss; ii) Who I most want to shag; iii) Why I'm going to leave. If the answers to i) and ii) are the same, you really should leave soon, if you haven't already been fired.

The dregs

Politics – Your mate's your mate. He's the one who'll be there through thick and thin, backing you up, cheering you on, standing you drinks. Do you really want to argue with him about the changing role of women in society, what the minimum wage should be, or the state of the global economy? You're in the pub! Lighten up.

Feelings – A difficult one this. You have feelings for your football team, for music, for your mate. But they're Man Feelings requiring no special language or expertise. Don't get sucked into the vortex of Women's Talk at any time, but especially not here, not now. Not unless you've had fourteen pints and are on a promise.

Illness – See above.

Mate's sister –You can guarantee that the one time your best mate will remember every word you said the night before is the occasion you unburden your undying love for his sister:

'You told me you want to Double Bass Katy, and Aussie kiss her budgie tongue.'

'Did I? Do I?'

Note: Confessions of incest are also to be avoided.

The Pub demands respect and there are a few crucial dos and don'ts of pub behaviour. While some of these are so blindingly obvious even a girl knows them, we feel that it is important that they are repeated just so that future generations will appreciate the complexities of our society. When a sociologist (huh) finds a copy of this book in 2520, our gift to posterity will be complete.

Not a coincidence that boxers fight in rounds. During WW1 it was made illegal to buy anyone but yourself a drink (after a soldier returned from the front to find 120 pints on the bar from his mates). Proof that government should never interfere with drinking.

Provision of credit by landlords – ruinous to both parties.

Serving of spirit chaser

The long pull – now known as the Happy Hour.

The drinking week

So, it's a Sunday afternoon in winter 1982. You've had six pints on the back of a masher of a hangover and are just getting into your stride. Shit, it's three o'clock – closing time … remember closing time? Last orders please? Bar is now closed – worse still, off licence is also now closed and there's only a bottle of cream sherry at home. Remember the Sunday Afternoon Desert? That weird Sunday afternoon blur? Queuing up at seven o'clock to get rid of your lunchtime hangover? If there's one thing we should be grateful for it is the end of the Sunday Lunchtime Dash – up until 1994, you had only three hours to bevvy (and that had generously been extended from two hours just a few years earlier) and three hours in the evening. Sunday was not a day of leisurely drinking, it was a day of getting as many down your neck as opening hours would permit. Sundays were speed-drinking days. Not anymore. Since all day opening on a Sunday came into being in 1994 and all-day everyday in 2005, the rhythm of the drinking week has changed.

Whereas the drinking highpoint of the week used to be Friday and Saturday nights (with a blip on Thursday night – pay day), we can now build a blissful drinking day on Sundays. It starts with a little pick-me-up just after opening hours (or even, la-di-da, a cappuccino), followed by the first pint. Lunch with a couple more and some football followed by dinner in the evening. All in the safety of your local with no prospect of unscrewing the lonely bottle of Harvey's Bristol Cream.

The Munich Beer Festival Oktoberfest
(actually in September – Germans so slapdash!)

As a reminder that it's not just us lager-spewing, knuckle-dusting Brits who are obsessed with beer, take a look at Munich. Every autumn they host the world's biggest piss-up and usually opulent streets become Rivers of Ralph and Hun-Huey Alley. The German government genuinely promotes the festival as a fun day out for all the family – complete, believe it or not, with fun fair. This is like the Dutch holding a skunk convention for paranoid schizophrenics. What could be better than sitting in a huge marquee with the missus and little ones, drinking beer by the litre (that's two pints by the way) before jumping into the waltzer and having an *Exorcist* moment on your seven year old, who returns the compliment, having just enjoyed his or her first Bierchen (little beer). In Lederhosen ...

Oh yes, when it comes to beer, the Germans are as Stone Age as us.

It's two weeks of utter mayhem – people are still missing from 1971 when it's rumoured that Jim Morrison turned up (two months after his 'death') until the festival finally put an end to him. No one here gets out alive, matey.

So, if you want to go and enjoy the fun ('spass' in German – we kid you not), how do you survive to tell the tale to your mates?

Train. Germans have a strict regime to work to; you should do the same. To get maximum enjoyment, you have to prepare clinically (of course) for the event. It's like their relentless success at penalty shoot-outs: in order to win (or have fun; it's all the same thing to them), you must *work*. Start drinking by the litre and monitor how long it is before you 'break the seal' (see page 33); with three thousand other people in the same tent you need to have 'reservoir bladder' to hold on to your seat.

Know your limits. Just because it looks like dissolved sherbet lemons doesn't mean it doesn't do the business.

Buy a T-shirt early on. It's a nice souvenir that doubles up as a barf bag.

Don't under any circumstances go on the rides. When you become SuperDrunk after a river of lager you think you can cope with 16 goes on the evil up and down and round and round machines. No. It doesn't work. What happens is that you release your inner self all over your unfortunate co-rider, who happily reciprocates the favour. It's mutually assured destruction.

If you are not capable of following the above guide, however, avoid the mayhem. There's always the Annual Elderflower Cordial Festival in Geneva where you can drink in neutral.

Beer and booze quotes

From *The Trumpet Major* by Thomas Hardy, a description of the perfect pint: 'It was of the most beautiful colour that the eye of an artist in beer could desire; full in body, yet brisk as a volcano; piquant, yet without a twang; luminous as an autumn sunset; free from streakiness of taste, but, finally, rather heady.'

'You can't be a real country unless you have a beer and an airline – it helps if you have some kind of a football team, or some nuclear weapons, but at the very least you need a beer.' Frank Zappa

[On drinking] 'Tis a pleasure of decayed fornicators, and the basest way of quenching love.' William Wycherley

'I have fed upon ale; I have eat my ale, drank my ale, and I always sleep upon ale.' George Farquhar

'Like other parties of the kind, it was first silent, then talky, then argumentative, then disputatious, then unintelligible, then altogethery, then inarticulate, and then drunk.' Lord Byron

'They who drink beer, will think beer.' Washington Irving

'What two ideas are more inseparable than beer and Britannia?' Sydney Smith

'If on my theme I rightly think / There are five reasons why men drink / Good wine, a friend, or being dry / Or lest we should be by-and-by / Or any other reason why.' Anon

'I am a character, You are a loose cannon, He is a drunk.' Craig Brown

Time, gentlemen, please!

So here we are. It's September. Leaves are falling outside. Late golden, summer light filters through the windows of Ye Olde Punchbowl, and through the two pints of Foxy's brew sitting in front of us. The sun brings out the rich, malty brown colours of the ale, and the creaminess of the foamy head, capping off perfection in a glass.

This is why we did it! This is why we're sitting here, less than a year since we had the insane idea of running our own pub, and brewing our own quality beer. It's been a mad few months but we wouldn't have missed it for the world. During the 'research' we've learnt more than we thought possible about beer, pubs and the amazing people who have kept the dream alive. There have been inspirations along the way. We met this fantastic boy, Sam, who is a master brewer and he's only 19 or 20. The guy's palette is amazing: he's like the Jilly Goolden of beer, but he's a Yorkshire lad.

It was the dream that, in an age where branding is king, where money talks and the small get squeezed out in a race for profits, there is still room for the craftsmen and women. The brewers who have a passion about their beer and a need to share it with an audience.

The dream that, among all the sports bars, the city centre meat markets and the global pubs with their sterile, marketed interiors and boil in the bag food, there was still room for the landlord who wants to provide something a bit different. Quality, seasonal menus, old pub games, great and unusual beers. The one-off pub giving customers something they can't get on every high street, something they'll travel miles for if necessary.

When all the joking's done, when we've gone through the stage of getting bollocksed every time we go out, that's what we want waiting for us – a haven. A home from home where we can escape to for a quiet pint,

have a leisurely Sunday lunch with family, or enjoy a great night out with our mates.

And we're glad to report that these places can be found all over the country. Maybe not in the numbers we'd like to see, but they're there. Of course they won't survive long without support, so make sure you get behind yours. And come and see us, next time you're around Harrogate.

Cheers!

Beer

Drinking

The Pub ☞ Food

Pub food, or 'do you want chips with that?'

In Europe there is still a long, sophisticated history of eating while you drink, while, in dear old Blighty, we've become wary of linking the acts, preferring to keep beer and kebab consumption as separate experiences. But this is recent. There's a long history of food in British pubs, and the act of eating something proper with your pint is finally enjoying the revival it deserves.

The Romans served food at fledgling 'pubs' and there was something to munch on while they drank, so it could be said that the Europeans introduced us to the joys of pub food – although invading Britain to do so was a bit over the top.

Then coaching inns of medieval times, which sprang up to cater for pilgrims, offered food along with drink and bedding. In the 19th century taverns also offered food and wine to those who could afford it: rich punters could bring a piece of meat into the tavern and have it cooked there for a penny.

In the Victorian public house, less sophisticated than the tavern, baked potatoes with cheese and mutton pies were the order of the day. It is from this fine fayre that our recent pub food culture derives.

By the 60s, the most you'd get in a pub was the option of a ploughman's lunch – a wedge of bread, slice of ham or cheese and a worn-out salad, usually with a huge dollop of Branston pickle on the side. Or you might find a Cornish pasty, garnished with some completely disposable cress.

Sometimes pubs serving 'real food' stretched to a white cheese or ham, or cheese *and* ham, bap that had been lovingly matured under a dirty plastic dome for a few days. These baps were generously topped with flour, most of which ended up on your trousers and round your lips, making you look like 'Bapface' – the English pub equivalent of a Colombian drug baron.

Just below the baps in the food chain were the jars of pickled eggs and pickled onions, which were certainly not designed to increase your chance of pulling, unless you were after a 'pork scratching' (see *Drinktionary* page 72).

In the late 60s, new drink-driving regulations were introduced and pubs had to start to cater for families and also provide their drinkers with something to soak up the booze. A frantic search for easy-to-cook 'traditional' pub food soon settled down into a menu of 'something frozen and chips'. Scampi, chicken, fish, sausages all came 'in a basket' (which simply meant 'we haven't got a dishwasher in the kitchen'). There was no escaping that salad garnish, though. This was gingerly moved to the overflowing ashtray, even though it was the only item on show not likely to have been frozen at some point.

This traditional 'fayre' (a culinary movement known as 'from freezer to fryer') continued through the 70s and into the 80s when the more adventurous pubs started to introduce European, Asian (i.e. Indian) and American-influenced 'dishes'. So lasagne, moussaka, chicken curry, chilli con carne and spaghetti bolognaise timidly started to creep on to menus. With chips, of course, in case we got scared.

Let's not forget that, even in the 80s, many pubs offered no 'real food' at all. Your options were peanuts – roasted or covered in marmite dust – or crisps. How we love crisps! We now eat a tonne of crisps every three minutes in the UK and the 80s were when crisps went mad. The Holy Trinity of ready salted, salt and vinegar or cheese and onion (still the nation's favourite) flavours were supplemented in an acid trip of invention, which culminated in the Day-glo cheesy Wotsit. In the decade of big hair, shoulder pads and red braces, pubs also gave you prawn cocktail crisps, which, if nothing else, were the very last word in additive-laden snacks.

Probably as a foolish bet, some far-seeing publican decided in 1991 that it would be a novel idea to reintroduce 'real' food to pubs, and the gastropub was born. The pub that invented the term (and, let's face it, it's not a particularly appetising one, is it?) is generally credited as being the Eagle in Clerkenwell, London.

Regardless of where it started, however, the gastropub is now everywhere. Your local (once the Red Lion but now the Ciabatta and Kumquat) wouldn't survive without 'traditional' unvarnished wooden tables and a menu with 'jus' written on it – and not as a spelling mistake. Things have definitely moved on. There's often a selection of genuinely interesting food and it is nearly always cooked from fresh on the premises. Top chefs cut their cooking teeth in such establishments. Some gastropubs are, admittedly, better than others. There are still a lot of boil-in-the-bag merchants out there, which somehow seems worse when you're claiming to serve good food, rather than any old rubbish.

Chips have become fries, or hand-cooked or twice-cooked, hand-hewn, potato wedges with their skins on; whatever their name, they don't automatically come with everything (but they often cost a fortune). You can even get a salad on its own – but now you can't throw the bits you don't like into an ashtray because, for better or worse, like the ploughman's, the ashtray is a relic of bygone days.

Some say that the gastropub isn't a pub at all, but a new kind of restaurant. We, however, think they're better than the high street barfing bars – buy six bottles get a bucket free – that have appeared alongside them. Recently there has been a shift in favour of a pub being a pub but with good food – whether the food is good bar snacks or excellent lunches and dinners – so less of a restaurant and more of a, well, pub. Which is where Ye Olde Punch Bowl comes in.

Real Ale
Real Food
Real Pub

Foxy's beer and food

When it comes to what to quaff with your food, you don't need to reach for the wine all the time. There are loads of beer alternatives which work as well or even better with different types of food than wine – and the joy of it is, of course, that you get to do lots of 'research' as you eat. Shame. There's no secret to any of this, it's just about what tastes on your plate and in your glass working well together. As we said in the beer tasting session, it's down to what your tongue tells you. Here are some ideas of what food to go with different beer styles, so start experimenting!

Wheat beers

Firstly, wheat beers do not look like beer. This is quite a good indicator of what is to come because they don't taste like traditional beer, either. Most wheat beers have a pastel, lemony hue which is the first indication of what they might taste like: light, citrussy and refreshing. The presence of coriander in some also gives a faint herbal quality. All this lemony zestiness and herbal freshness has fish written all over it. But this is only half the story, because this food-loving beer will match many food styles from Thai and Malaysian to Italian iced desserts (okay, Cornetto). The citrus and herbal element marries perfectly with the lemongrass, Kaffir lime leaf and coriander used in South East Asian cuisine. Wheat beers are also a great fan of poultry – particularly with herb-based sauces.

Best with:
Asian prawn noodle salad
   Whitby cod with Asian spices
      Scotch egg (yes, honestly!)
         Lemon meringue pie

Trappist and Abbey

The Trappist beers are still solely made by Monks within the abbey walls, and are truly artisan products of the highest value. Let's face it, what better bloke to prepare your brew than someone with no distractions from the likes of girls, mind-altering substances and on-line poker. And although they are brewing on a commercial basis, the dollar is not their God. Abbey beers tend to be copies of these, albeit damn good ones. While there are a few sub-styles within this category, namely dubbels and trippels, one word can sum up the whole genre: complexity – great big, dark, fruity, alcohol-laden, extraordinary complexity. Flavours rise and fall in fleeting seconds and they just keep coming. In the case of dubbels, the dark, plummy flavours lend themselves to rich stews and sweeter meats such as lamb and duck where the sweet caramel flavours in the beer compare with similar flavours generated from the caramelised fat of the meat. Trippels are lighter in colour and stronger in alcohol. Rather surprisingly, they go fabulously well with pesto, where the intense flavours of basil, garlic and Parmesan can stand up to their complex intensity. When it comes to the super-strength dark strong ales, you need super-strength, dark strong food to match the intensity of flavour: venison, pigeon, braised oxtail are all contenders, as are big-flavoured cheeses.

Best with:
Steak and kidney pud
   Venison and juniper pie
      Stinking Bishop cheese
        Roly poly pudding

Fruit Beers

There's nothing alcopop about these beers. Fermented in open vessels by wild yeasts in the atmosphere, they pre-date the discovery of yeast itself. From real fruit macerated for several months, to oak cask maturation, these beers are about as artisan as you can get. The perfect balance of sweet and sour makes them an ideal partner for game – particularly venison and pigeon that have a natural affinity for soft fruit. They are a vastly cheaper alternative to Sauternes as an accompaniment to chicken livers and other offal. But it's when they're matched with desserts that they come into their own. The flavours work well with fruit-based desserts and fruit coulis. Chocolate matches perfectly, particularly with the cherry and raspberry beers, while the subtle sourness contrasts with the sweetness of many other desserts.

Best with:
Mature Brie
   English trifle
      Sun-dried tomato and basil tart
         Spiced turkey stew with cranberries

English Ales

This covers an awesome range of bottled, bottled-conditioned, cask and keg ales. The real artisan products in this genre however are bottle-conditioned and cask-conditioned, such as top fermented brews where live yeast in the bottle or cask continues to give character and complexity to the beer long after it has left the brewery. Within these two categories there are many different styles generating all manner of different aromas and flavours from intense tropical fruitiness to freshly cut hay. But there are certain characteristics of English ale that run through many of the different types i.e. bitters, pale ales, milds and strong ales. These are essentially: caramel sweetness, hoppy bitterness, and varying degrees of fruitiness. It's no coincidence that our traditional classic dishes are perfect matches for these styles of beer. Roast beef and Yorkshire pudding, roast leg of lamb, slow-cooked belly pork, Welsh rarebit, apple crumble have their traditions steeped in the grain rather than the grape. Throw in the stews, casseroles and game dishes and there are very few good British meals that don't suit quality British ale.

Best with:
Traditional Sunday lunches of roasts with all the trimmings
   Lancashire hotpot
      Mutton stew

Stout and Porter

Toasted caramel, chocolate and astringent bitterness are hallmarks of these richly dark beers. From shellfish such as lobster and oyster, where their bitterness offers a dynamic contrast with the sweetness of the meat, to rich chocolate desserts. Matched up with Christmas pudding, the beer brings out the fruit in all its glory, while the food brings out the malty beer flavours.

Best with:
Chocolate brownies (especially chocolate stout)
   Fish pie
      Moules Mariniere

Pilsner

These beers are floral, honeyed and buttery. Their crisp, dry carbonation makes them the ultimate beverage for drinking with oily fish such as salmon, mackerel and tuna. They'll cut through deep-fried food like a knife through butter, and cleanse the palate more effectively than the spritziest mineral waters, or wines when drunk with spicy ethnic cuisines. Not surprisingly, Pilsners are also great with food from their native Eastern Europe. Crack open a bottle when you next eat Chicken Kiev and you'll discover a match made in Heaven.

Best with:
Chicken Tikka Masala
   Lamb Tagine
      Fish and chips
         Deep-fried onions

Keep experimenting, tasting and trusting those gut instincts, and before long you'll have a stunning beer and food matching repertoire. And if you begin to sound like an expert, the ladies might just let you keep that cupboardful of beer – for research purposes, obviously.

Foxy's Beer recipes

Last night's leftover pizza with curry sauce is no way to woo the fair lady. Here are my tried-and-tested dishes to guarantee some kitchen love-action (just turn the oven off first).

Toad in the hole

SERVES 3–4

Food and beer combos don't come much better than this – just make sure you use the best quality sausages you can get your hands on.

110g	plain flour
2	eggs
200ml	milk
85ml	good British ale, such as Timothy Taylor's Landlord
	salt and pepper
4 tbsp	vegetable oil
6	top-notch sausages
	salt and pepper

1 Preheat the oven to 220°C/400°F/Gas mark 6. For the batter, sift the flour and seasoning into a large bowl. Make a well in the centre and break in the eggs. Add half the milk and whisk with an electric whisk until smooth. Add the remaining milk, whisk again then pour in the beer and stir until combined. When the batter is smooth, cover the bowl with a clean tea towel or plate and rest for about 30 minutes.

2 Pour 2 tablespoons of vegetable oil into a large frying pan and cook the sausages until they're golden brown. Transfer to a roasting tin measuring 28 x 18cm. Put the tin over a medium heat, pour in the remaining oil and heat until it is almost smoking.

3 Pour the batter into the tin around the sausages and bake for 20 minutes or until the batter has risen and is golden brown.

Guinness stew

SERVES 4

This heart-warming bowl of beery cheer can be transformed into the ultimate steak pie by simply putting the finished stew into heat-proof dishes and wacking on a lid of ready-rolled puff pastry – genius!

1.25kg	stewing beef, cut into 4cm cubes
400ml	Guinness
3 cloves	garlic, crushed
3 tbsp	plain flour, seasoned with salt and pepper
3 tbsp	vegetable oil
2	carrots, sliced
2	onions, sliced
1 tbsp	tomato purée
1	sprig of thyme
1	bay leaf
350ml	beef stock
	salt and pepper

1 Put the beef, beer and garlic into a large, flat-bottomed pan and marinate overnight in the refrigerator. Preheat the oven to 140°C/275°F/ Gas mark 1. Drain the beef, reserving the marinade. Pat the meat dry on kitchen paper and toss it in the seasoned flour. Shake off any excess.

2 Heat the oil in a heavy-based casserole dish and fry the beef in batches until golden brown. Remove the meat with a slotted spoon and set aside. Add the vegetables and fry for 10 minutes or until they start to colour. Add the tomato purée. Continue to fry for another couple of minutes, stirring all the time.

3 Add the browned beef and the reserved marinade and bring to a simmer, scraping up any browned bits from the bottom of the pan. Season with salt and pepper, add the thyme, bay leaf and stock and bring to the boil. Remove from the heat, cover and cook in the oven for two hours.

Slow roast lamb shank with beer mustard mash

SERVES 4

This is ultimate comfort food. Crack open a strong old ale, such as Bellhaven, settle down in front of the footie and you'll wonder what was ever depressing about cold, rainy nights.

4	lamb shanks
1 tbsp	vegetable oil
500g	carrots, roughly chopped
1	onion, roughly chopped
1	stick of celery, roughly chopped
500ml	good quality, fruity ale such as Bellhaven
500ml	lamb stock
	sprig of thyme
	sprig of rosemary
1	bay leaf
	salt and pepper

For the mash:

500g	potatoes, preferably Maris Piper, cut into quarters
200ml	good ale such as Greene King IPA
	pinch of salt
75g	unsalted butter, softened
100ml	milk
	white pepper and salt to taste
2 tsp	whole grain mustard
	vegetable oil for frying

1 Preheat the oven to 150°C/300°F/Gas mark 2. Season the shanks with salt and pepper. Heat the oil in a large ovenproof saucepan and brown the lamb shanks on all sides. Set the lamb aside and fry the carrots, onion and celery until lightly browned.

2 Return the shanks to the pan and pour over the beer and stock. Bring to a simmer then add the herbs. Cover and place in the oven for two and a half hours – or until the meat easily falls away from the bone.

3 When cooked, remove the shanks and set aside, keeping them warm. Strain the cooking liquor into a clean pan and boil to reduce to a gravy consistency.

4 To make the mash, place the potatoes in a medium pan and just cover with water. Add the beer and salt, bring to the boil and simmer until soft. Drain well and steam off any residual water. Pass through a sieve while still hot and add the butter and milk. Add the mustard and season well.

5 To serve, place a dollop of mash in the centre of the plate. Put the whole shank on top of the mash.

Beer and onion gravy

1 tbsp	vegetable oil
1	large onion, thinly sliced
125ml	good British ale such as Marston's Pedigree
2 tsp	plain flour
1 tsp	tomato purée
300ml	beef stock

1 Heat the oil in a heavy-based saucepan then add the onion. Fry gently until soft and golden brown. Pour in the beer and stir for a minute until the onions have absorbed the beer. Add the tomato purée and fry for a further minute, stirring all the time. Stir in the flour and fry for a couple more minutes before finally adding the beef stock a little at a time, whisking until smooth.

Stilton, ale and caramelised onion tarts

SERVES 4

This may sound all posh and complicated but it's actually easy as pie –
and guarantees bankable love points! If you can't be bothered making
the pastry, just buy the ready-rolled shortcrust from the supermarket.

For the pastry:

50g	unsalted butter, but extra for greasing
100g	plain flour, plus extra for dusting
50g	unsalted butter
	pinch of salt
25m	full-flavoured ale such as Old Speckled Hen

For the filling:

1 tbsp	vegetable oil
10g	butter
2	onions, finely sliced
25ml	full-flavoured ale, as above
2	eggs
10fl oz	double cream
100g	Stilton, crumbled into small pieces

1 Preheat the oven to 180°C/350°F/Gas mark 4. Lightly grease a 21cm
diameter tart tin. Make the pastry by blitzing all the ingredients together
in a food processor for a few seconds. Turn onto a floured work surface
and knead together until the mixture forms a smooth dough. Wrap tightly
in cling film and rest in the refrigerator for 30 minutes.

2 In the meantime, heat the oil and butter in a medium frying pan, then
add the onions and fry gently for 15 minutes or until golden brown. Add
the beer, remove from the heat and leave to stand for a few seconds until
the onions have absorbed most of the beer. Beat the eggs and then add to
the onion and beer mixture with the double cream.

3 Roll the pastry out on a lightly floured surface as thinly as possible and then fit into the tart tin. Leave the excess pastry overhanging. Cut a circle of non-stick baking paper large enough to line the pastry case.

4 Place the paper over the pastry and add a handful of dried baking beans or uncooked rice to secure. Blind bake the pastry for 10 minutes. Remove, the tart, discard the blind baking beans, then return to the oven for another 6 minutes or until the pastry is cooked and lightly golden.

5 Spoon the filling mixture to the brim of the pastry and crumble the Stilton into each tart. Return to the oven for 5 minutes, or until bubbling and golden brown. Allow to cool slightly, then trim off the excess pastry. Serve immediately, or cool, refrigerate and serve cold.

Beer butt chicken (yes, seriously)

Here's one to impress the potential in-laws with your culinary skills. Serve it upright with the can still intact for maximum impact!

1	chicken
1 can	good Pilsner such as Urquell or Budvar
25g	butter
	salt and pepper

1 Preheat the oven to 180°C/350°F/Gas mark 4. Season the inside and outside of the chicken and rub the butter over the skin. Crack open the tinny, and drink about half of it. Open up the chicken's jacksy and insert the can – open end first.

2 Sit the chicken upright on an oven tray using the tin as the third leg of a tripod, pushing forward the chicken legs as the other two supports. The beer helps keep the chicken moist while infusing it with beery flavour. Roast for about 50 minutes, or until the chicken is fully cooked through. You can check the 'doneness' by inserting a skewer into the flesh. If the juices run clear, the bird is cooked.

Chicken tagine

SERVES 4

Packed with exotic North African flavours – it goes down a storm with a bottle of Morocco ale from Yorkshire's Daleside brewery.

1 tbsp	oil for frying
1 kg	chicken thighs
2	onions, chopped
2	cloves garlic, chopped
1 tsp	ground ginger
1 tsp	ground coriander
1½ tsp	ground cumin
1½ tsp	ground cinnamon
150m	water
150ml	blonde ale such as Morrissey and Foxy's
1 tsp	turmeric
125g	dried apricots
125g	sultanas
1½ tbsp	honey

1 Heat the oil in a large frying pan and brown the chicken on all sides. Remove and set aside. Gently fry the onions and garlic until soft. Add all the ground spices and cook out for a couple more minutes. Return the chicken to the frying pan and add the water, beer and turmeric.

2 Bring to a simmer, turn down the heat and cover the pan. Simmer gently for 30 minutes. Put the apricots in a small bowl, cover with cold water and leave to soak for 30 minutes. Drain and add the fruit, and honey to the tagine then simmer for a further 15 minutes. Serve with couscous and some flaked roasted almonds.

Quick lamb curry

SERVES 4

**This fiery little bad boy gives you the taste of the takeaway at home.
Try a sexy Indian lager such as Kingfisher for the 'full monty'
dining experience.**

1kg	boneless lamb chump, cut into 3cm cubes and marinated overnight in a bottle of beer, such as Marston's Old Empire.
2 tbsp	oil
2	onions, finely diced
2	cloves garlic
½ tsp	ground ginger
1 tsp	turmeric
1 tsp	dried chilli flakes
1 tsp	ground cumin
1 tsp	tomato purée
700ml	lamb stock or stock cube
2	tomatoes, roughly chopped
2 tsp	fresh coriander, finely chopped
	salt and pepper

1 Dry the lamb cubes thoroughly and reserve 100ml of the marinating liquor. Place the oil in a frying pan and heat until sizzling, then add the lamb cubes. Season with salt and pepper and brown quickly on all sides. Remove from the pan and set aside.

2 Fry the onions and garlic for a couple of minutes in the same pan, then add the spices and tomato purée. Cook for a couple of minutes stirring constantly, then blend with the stock and reserved marinade. Add the chopped tomatoes and simmer for 5 minutes. Remove from the heat, stir in the chopped coriander and serve.

Chunky salmon and pea fish cakes with wheat beer mayo

SERVES 4

How often have fish cakes tasted more like fish-flavoured potato cakes? This recipe is designed to redress the balance, and gives you the best excuse to crack open an artisan wheat beer in the process

½ tbsp	wheat beer such as Hoegaarden
1 tbsp	mayonnaise
175g	potatoes, cut into even sized chunks
50g	frozen peas
250g	salmon fillet, cut into 1cm cubes
2 tsp	chopped flat leaf parsley
60g	fine polenta
1 tbsp	vegetable oil
	salt and pepper for seasoning

1 Preheat the oven to 180°C/350°F/Gas mark 4. Place a large baking tray in the oven to warm. To make the wheat beer mayo, put the beer and mayo in a small bowl and mix well. Place the potatoes in a medium saucepan and cover with cold water. Bring to the boil and simmer until the potatoes are cooked through. Drain, mash and reserve. Cook the peas for a couple of minutes in boiling water and refresh under cold water until cool.

2 Combine the mayonnaise, mash, peas, salmon and chopped parsley in a bowl and season. Shape the mixture into patties. Place the polenta on a large plate. Dip the patties into the polenta, gently removing any excess.

3 Heat the oil in a large frying pan and fry the fish cakes for a few minutes on each side until golden brown. Transfer to the warmed baking tray and place in the oven for 8 minutes, or until piping hot and cooked through. Remove and serve.

Quick Welsh rarebit with stout poached egg

MAKES 4 SLICES

Get this! You can make the poached eggs in advance by taking them out of the pan when they're just a little under, and put them straight into iced water. Keep them in the fridge and then bob back into very hot water for a few minutes to re-heat. Would you believe it?

250g	mature Cheddar cheese, grated
100ml	stout or porter such as Fuller's London Porter
1 tsp	English mustard powder
1	egg yolk
	a few drops of Worcesteshire sauce
4	slices of bread
2 litres	water
500ml	beer such as Old Speckled Hen
4	large eggs

1 Mix the cheese, stout or porter, mustard, egg yolk and Worcestershire sauce together in a bowl, or ideally, blitz in a food processor to a paste.

2 Toast the bread on both sides and then spread the mixture in a thick layer, making sure you cover the crusts, too.

3 Meanwhile, place the water and the stout or porter in a large saucepan and heat until simmering. Give it a swirl with a fork or whisk and gently crack in the eggs. Cook for 4 minutes, or until the yolks are runny and the whites firm.

4 Keep the liquid at a simmer and skim off any scum that forms on the surface. Lift out the eggs and rinse quickly under hot water. Meanwhile, grill the rarebit until it turns golden brown. Serve immediately, topped with the egg.

Beer battered fish

SERVES 4

Crunchy, crispy batter coating fresh, succulent, flakey, white-fleshed fish – what else is there to want for in life – apart from a cracking beer to go with it?!

200g self raising flour
300ml good quality ale, well chilled, such as Worthington White Shield
50g plain flour, for dusting the fish
2 litres vegetable oil for deep frying
4 good sized haddock or pollack fillets
salt and pepper

1 Sift the self raising flour into a medium bowl then whisk in the beer, a little at a time, and keep whisking until you have a smooth batter. Season with the salt and pepper.

2 Season the fish and dust with plain flour, patting off any excess. Dip the fish in the batter to coat.

3 Pour the vegetable oil into a large heavy-based saucepan ensuring the oil doesn't reach more than halfway up. Heat the oil to about 190°C. To test, drop a small piece of bread into the oil: if it sizzles quickly, the oil is hot enough to start frying. Carefully lower the fish into the oil and fry for 4 to 5 minutes or until the batter is a golden. You may have to do this in two batches.

Mini Scotch eggs

MAKES 4

If you think of Scotch eggs as a last attempt to get some stomach lining after a Friday night out, try my top posh version.

4 tbsp	eggs cooked for 7 minutes in boiling water, refreshed under cold water, shells removed
1 tbsp	oil
1	small onion, finely chopped
1 clove	garlic, crushed
1 tsp	thyme, finely chopped
50ml	full flavoured ale, such as Shepherd Neame's Bishops Finger
300g	pork mince
1 tsp	parsley, finely chopped
4 tbsp	seasoned plain flour
2	eggs, lightly whisked
4oz	fresh white breadcrumbs
	vegetable oil, for deep frying

1 Heat the oil in a frying pan and add the onion, garlic and thyme. Pour in the beer, and cook for a couple more minutes until it has been fully absorbed into the onion mixture. Set aside to cool. Combine the pork mince and parsley in a bowl, then add to the onion and beer mixture. Divide the mixture into 4 and use to coat the cooked eggs.

2 Place the seasoned flour, whisked eggs and breadcrumbs in separate bowls. Roll each egg in the flour, patting off any excess. Coat in the eggs, then the breadcrumbs.

3 Pour the oil into a deep sided frying pan (don't fill the pan more than half full with oil), and heat until a cube of white bread browns in 45 seconds. Carefully lower the Scotch eggs into the oil and deep fry for about 7 minutes until golden brown.

Steak and kidney on toast with beery cream sauce

SERVES 2

Who needs pie when you've got toast? This is a fab teatime snack or luxury Sunday brunch – and it's great way to use up those leftover beer dregs.

1 tbsp	vegetable oil
60g	bacon lardons
800g	chicken livers, cleaned and trimmed
100ml	Oak aged beer such as Innis & Gunn beer
200ml	double cream
1 tbsp	fresh parsley, finely chopped
	salt and pepper
4	slices thick white bread

1 Put the oil in a small frying pan and gently fry the bacon lardons until golden brown. Remove, drain on kitchen paper and set aside. Season the chicken livers and fry on a high heat for a couple of minutes on each side until golden brown. Drain on kitchen paper and keep warm.

2 Add the beer and cream to the frying pan, bring gently to the boil then cook for a couple of minutes. Add the bacon and chopped parsley and season. Toast the bread, arrange the livers on top and pour over the sauce.

Chunky chilli

SERVES 6

For a quicker version, just substitute the braising steak for mince and forget about the marinating.

300g	braising steak, cut into 1cm squares
100ml	strong, full-flavoured beer such as Marston's Pedigree
1 tbsp	vegetable oil
500g	minced beef
1	onion, finely chopped
2 cloves	garlic, crushed
30g	red chillies, finely chopped
1 tsp	hot chilli powder
2 tsp	tomato purée
1 x 400g tin	chopped tomatoes
1 x 400g tin	kidney beans, drained of liquid
	salt and pepper

1 Put the steak in a medium bowl, pour the beer over it, cover and place in the refrigerator overnight.

2 Drain the beef, reserving the marinating liquid and pat dry with kitchen paper. Heat the oil in a frying pan and fry the beef until it browns. Remove from the pan and set aside. Brown the mince in the same pan, and set aside with the braising steak including any meat juices.

3 To make the chilli, fry the onion, garlic and chopped chillies for a few minutes until they start to soften. Add the chilli powder and carry on frying for a couple more minutes. Keep stirring so the mixture doesn't burn on the bottom of the pan.

4 Add the tomato purée and fry for a couple more minutes, stirring constantly. Put the meat back in the pan along with the tinned tomatoes and the reserved marinating liquor, and simmer very gently for at least an hour and a half or until the meat is tender. Add the drained kidney beans 15 minutes before the end of cooking.

Mozzarella, pesto and roasted red pepper toasties

MAKES ABOUT 14 CANAPÉ SIZED PORTIONS

This is great party food – no cutlery, no crockery, no washing up! It will also endear you to the veggie contingent – hey! you never know!

50ml	olive oil, plus extra for greasing
7	slices of medium white sliced bread, crusts removed
1	red bell pepper
2	rounds of buffalo mozzarella, cut into 1 cm slices

For the pesto:

1 clove	garlic
30g	pine nuts
100g	basil, thick stalks removed
1 tbsp	beer (Belgian Tripel beer such as Westmalle or Leffe)
30g	freshly grated Parmesan

1 Lightly oil a 14-hole mini-tart tin. Preheat the oven to 180°C/350°F/Gas mark 4. To make the toasties, roll out each slice of bread until wafer thin. With a round cutter, cut out two circles from each slice of bread. Press the bread into the holes to form a shallow 'bread basket'. Brush each piece with a little olive oil and bake for 8–10 minutes, or until lightly coloured. Allow to cool, and then store in an airtight container.

2 Retain oven temperature. Place the whole pepper on a baking tray and roast until the skin turns black, turning a couple of times during cooking. Remove from the oven, transfer to a small bowl and cover with clingfilm.

3 When cool, peel away the clingfilm and discard the skin, drain off the liquid and remove and discard the seeds. Slice the pepper into thin strips, and set aside. Cut the mozzarella into slices about 1cm thick and set aside.

4 Blitz all the pesto ingredients in a food processor. Place the mozzarella inside the bread cases. Top with a dollop of pesto and then finish with a couple of strips of roasted red pepper.

Asian prawn noodle salad

SERVES 4

Try serving this with a cloudy Belgian wheat beer such as Hoegaarden – it's made with coriander and curacao orange peel – perfect complimentary flavours for a spot of spicy Asian cuisine.

Dressing:
2 sticks	lemongrass, roughly chopped
2 cloves	garlic, finely chopped
5	large red chillies, finely chopped
50ml	Thai fish sauce (Nam Pla)
100ml	Hoegaarden
50ml	white wine vinegar
60g	caster sugar
	juice of 2 limes
150g	rice noodles
	bunch of chopped coriander
400g	juicy cooked prawns

1 To make the dressing, place the first 7 ingredients in a medium saucepan and heat without simmering. Remove from heat and allow to cool. Discard the lemongrass and add the lime juice. Prepare the noodles according to the packet instructions.

2 Combine the dressing with the noodles, then add the chopped coriander and prawns.

Sausage and mash burger

MAKES 4 HEFTY BURGERS

This recipe will win friends and influence people – and cement your status as undisputed barbecue king of the world.

600g	minced pork
1	small onion, finely chopped
3 cloves	garlic, crushed
2 tsp	parsley, chopped
2 tsp	sage, chopped
30g	fresh breadcrumbs
	salt and pepper to taste
75ml	beer
1	egg
180g	beer mash (See page 128.)

1 Make the burger mix by simply combining all the ingredients, except the mash, and then refrigerate the mixture for up to 12 hours. It's much easier to handle when cold and firm.

2 When you're ready to assemble, divide the pork mixture into 8 and make a well in the middle of each one. Divide the mash equally between 4 of the patties pressing it into the well.

3 Place another pattie on top of each mash-filled one and seal around the edges, shaping into a burger as you do. To cook, simply brush with oil and barbecue in the usual manner.

Garlic tip: Remove the root from inside the garlic clove as it can cause indigestion and be bitter. Also, sprinkle salt over the garlic and leave for a few seconds before crushing, as this helps break it down more easily.

Hoegaarden and peach semi-freddo

MAKES 8 RAMEKINS

Invite her back for one of these and she'll instantly thaw out! Sounds impressive, but it's actually a great way to cheat at ice-cream. There's no churning, cooking or aggravation, just a smooth and awesomely tasty frozen dessert. You'll need eight little ramekin dishes (little white pots).

4 egg yolks
75g caster sugar
425g tin of peaches
100ml wheat beer such as Hoegaarden or Paulaner
45g icing sugar
250ml double cream
2 egg whites

1 Lightly beat the egg yolks and caster sugar until they are smooth and pale. Drain the tinned peaches and purée with the beer and icing sugar in a food processor.

2 Whip the cream until it thickens to the point where it just holds its form; whisk the egg whites until they form soft peaks. Mix all the ingredients together, gently folding in the whisked egg whites. Pour into the ramekins and leave to set in the freezer for at least 4–5 hours.

Ramekin tip: If you don't have ramekins, you can use a shallow dish. This may take longer to freeze than individual dishes.

Mini Beer Chocolate Tarts

Here's one to impress the ladies – who knows where some well spent time in the kitchen could lead?

15	mini sweet pastry cases
200g	good quality dark chocolate (min 70% cocoa solids)
100g	unsalted butter
75ml	strong Belgian ale
3	egg yolks
1	egg
50g	sugar

1 Preheat the oven to 220°C/425°F/Gas mark 7. Bring a saucepan of water to a gentle simmer and sit a heatproof bowl over the top – don't allow the water to come into contact with the bottom of the bowl.

2 Break the chocolate into the bowl and add the butter and the beer. While the chocolate mixture is melting, whisk the eggs and the sugar until pale and smooth. When the chocolate has melted, stir the mixture until the ingredients are combined.

3 Tip into the egg and sugar mixture, stir well and pour into the tart cases. Bake for 4 minutes. Allow to cool, then refrigerate overnight and serve. Anyone fancy a tart?

Directory

There are an amazing number of specialist beer shops, home-brew businesses, and internet mail order companies in the UK. Here is but a smattering of them. The internet is also a brilliant resource for those wanting to learn more about beer and brewing, with discussion groups giving tips on good brewing technique, tastings and beer festivals.

Home-brew suppliers

These guys will set you up with all the ingredients and kit you need to make your own brew. They're also a great source of knowledge when you're having trouble sparging your wort.

The Brewshop

The Brewshop is a specialist supplier of home-brew ingredients and equipment that has been trading over 30 years. Shop by internet or visit their premises in Stockport.
48 Buxton Rd, Heaviley, Stockport,
Nr Manchester, Cheshire, UK
Tel: 0161 480 4880
www.thebrewshop.com

Warminster Maltings

Warminster Maltings supplies an extensive range of malts, extracts and brewing ingredients for home-brewers and commercial brewers.
39 Pound Street, Warminster, Wiltshire
BA12 8NN UK
Tel: 01985 212014
www.warminster-malt.co.uk/news.html

Brew it yourself

Internet-only retailers of a wide range of home-brewing kit.
www.brew-it-yourself.co.uk

Art of Brewing

An online home-brew shop for all home-brewers, mashers, craft brewers and country wine makers in the UK.
Tel: 020 8397 2111
www.art-of-brewing.co.uk

Easy Brew

A well-established family-run business supplying a wide range of home-brewing products and equipment throughout the United Kingdom.
Tel: 01425 479972
www.easybrew.co.uk

Cellars Brewers and Winemakers Supplies

Established in 1979. Many years of experience in all forms of brewing, they cater to everyone from beginners to the very experienced.
Canton House, 451 Cowbridge Road East, Canton, Cardiff CF5 1JH, UK
Tel: 029 2066 5867
www.homebrewwales.co.uk

Good beer stockists

These guys are beer heroes who do the hard work of sourcing amazing brews from around the world and making them available to you for a small price. The range of ales on these websites and in these shops is awesome! Keep an eye out for the specialist offies promoting local brews – hmm, delicious. Beer University, here we come!

MAIL ORDER SUPPLIERS

Beer 4 Home
An online beer shop delivering draught real cask ale to drink from 19 craft breweries.
Tel: 0800 6349938
www.beer4home.co.uk

Beer Ritz Ltd
Stocks a wide range of real ales, imported lagers, stouts and fruit beers from around the world.
Tel: 01423 359371
www.beerritz.co.uk

Realale.com
Established in early 2005. They stock a wide range of real ales, ciders, perries (pear ciders) and beers produced by British microbreweries. They also have a London shop.
Tel: 020 8892 3710
www.realale.com

Only fine beer
The website lists over a thousand beers and ciders from 50 countries around the world.
Tel: 01245 362950
www.onlyfinebeer.co.uk

Beer Here
Another great selection of beers from all over the globe. Also stock extras like aprons, gift packs and glasses.
Tel: 01706 718095
www.beerhere.co.uk

LONDON

Uto beer
London SE1
A specialist drinks company selling beers from around the world.
Tel: 020 7378 9461
www.utobeer.co.uk

Real Ale
371 Richmond Road, London, Twickenham, London TW1 2EF
Tel: 020 8822 3710
www.realale.com

NORTH

Ale Cellar
An extensive selection of beers and gift packs from around the world. Online service and shop.
24 Woodland Terrace, Darlington, County Durham DL3 9NU
Tel: 01325 252022
www.alecellar.com

Jug and Bottle
An award-winning, independent real ale off-licence. The shop opened in 2002, and sells real ale and cider to take away in jugs and has a vast array of bottled beer, cider and perry from around the world.
The Old School, Main Street, Bubwith, East Riding of Yorkshire YO8 6LX
Tel: 01757 289707
www.jugandbottle.co.uk

The Archer Road Beer Stop

Archer Road Beer Stop dispenses draught real ale in a variety of containers and quantities ranging from a few pints to an entire nine-gallon cask straight from the brewery. They also stock an excellent selection of bottled beers.

Archer Road Beer Stop, 57 Archer Road, Sheffield s8 0jt Tel: 0114 255 1356

The York Beer and Wine Shop

Over 250 beers from around the world, including strong British element and cask-conditioned ales. Opened in 1985.

28 Sandringham Street, Fishergate, York YO10 4BA Tel: 01904 647136
www.yorkbeerandwineshop.co.uk

MIDLANDS

The Offie

142 Clarendon Park Road, Leicester LE2 3AE Tel: 01509 413970
www.the-offie.co.uk

CA Rookes Wine Merchants

7 Western Road Estate, Stratford-upon-Avon, Warwickshire CV37 0AH
Tel: 01789 297777
www.carookes.co.uk

EAST

Beers of Europe

Fourteen thousand square feet of purpose-built shop and warehouse stacked with more than 150,000 bottles of UK Ales, World Beers, and more besides. Also home-brew kit.

Beers of Europe Ltd, Garage Lane, Setchey, King's Lynn, Norfolk PE33 0BE Tel: 01553 812000
www.beersofeurope.co.uk

The Real Ale Shop

Stocks over 50 ales made in Norfolk microbreweries.

Branthill Farm, Wells-next-the-sea, Norfolk NR23 1SB
Tel: 01328 710810
www.therealaleshop.co.uk

SOUTH EAST

The Beer Essentials

Stocks over 150 beers including many English and local brews.

The Beer Essentials, 30a East Street, Horsham, West Sussex RH12 1H2
Tel: 01403 218890
www.thebeeressentials.co.uk

Trafalgar wines

Has over 60 types of beer from around the world including fruit beers.

Trafalgar Street, Brighton BN1 4EQ
Tel: 01273 683325

The Bitter End

Over 500 beers from all over the UK.

139 Masons Hill, Bromley, Kent BR2 9HY
Tel: 020 8466 6083
www.thebitterend.biz

SOUTH WEST

Corks of Cotham

54 Cotham Hill, Bristol BS6 6JX
Tel: 0117 9731620
www.corksof.com

Tuckers Maltings

Teign Road, Newton Abbott, Devon TQ12 4AA
Tel: 01626 334734
tuckersonline.co.uk

SCOTLAND

JL Gill
*A selection of bottled beers from every
brewery in Scotland.*
26 West High Street, Crieff,
Perthshire PH7 4DL
Tel: 01764 652396
www.scottishproduce.co.uk

John Scott & Miller
Wide choice of Scottish and world beers.
15–19 Bridge Street, Kirkwall, Orkney
KW15 1HR
Tel: 01856 873146
www.jsmorkney.co.uk

NORTHERN IRELAND

The Vineyard
*Over 200 beers from around the world,
including UK and Ireland.*
375–377 Ormeau Road, Belfast
BT7 3GP
Tel: 028 9064 5774
www.vineyardbelfast.co.uk

WALES

Phillip Morgan & Sons
7 Spring Gardens, Narbeth,
Pembrokeshire SA67 7BP
TEL: 01834 862200

IRELAND

Realbeers.ie
*RealBeers.ie is owned by Real Beers Ltd, an
Irish company based in Dublin. A fine
selection of beers from all over the world
are available by mail order.*
Real Beers Ltd, MG Building, Unit 12,
Ladyswell Road, Mulhuddart, Dublin 15,
Ireland
Tel: 00 353 1 5240152
www.realbeers.ie.

Redmonds Off Licence
Over 100 bottled beers in stock.
25 Ranelagh, Dublin 6, Ireland
Tel: 00 353 1 497 1739
www.redmonds.ie

Traditional pub games

**Why not create that perfect pub
environment at home, by installing a
traditional pub game like bar billiards
or Ringing the Bull in your Living
Room? Quality! These guys can
help you...**

Masters Games
*Traditional games including bar billiards,
Shove Ha' Penny and Aunt Sally
manufactured for use in pubs.*
www.mastersgames.com
01727 855058.
custserv@mastersgames.com

Web resources

Pub is the Hub
Pub is the Hub was set up in 2001 through the Rural Action Programme of Business in the Community. It encourages breweries, pub owners, licensees and local communities to work together to help retain and enhance rural pubs.
www.pubisthehub.org.uk/pithlive/res/publications/index.html

Beer Expert.co.uk
A mine of information on brewing, beer and pubs.
www.beerexpert.co.uk

CAMRA (Campaign for Real Ale)
CAMRA campaigns for real ale, real pubs and consumer rights. It is an independent, voluntary organisation with over 89,000 members. A great source of information for everything ale-related.
www.camra.org.uk

Beer festivals

If, after all this, you can't be bothered to give brewing a go yourself, why not check out the real ale festivals that happen all year round all over the country? Dates vary from year-to-year.

JANUARY
National Winter Ales Festival
www.winterales.uku.co.uk
Atherton Bent Bongs Beer Bash
www.bentnbongs.com
Burton winter festival
www.burtoncamra.org.uk
Cambridge winter festival
www.cambridge-camra.org.uk/waf
Chelmsford winter festival
www.chelmsfordcamra.org.uk
Derby Twelfth Night Festival
www.derbycamra.org.uk
Exeter winter festival
www.exetercamra.org.uk
Pendle beer festival
www.pendlebeerfestival.co.uk
St Neots winter festival
www.huntscamra.org.uk/festivals/stneots

FEBRUARY
Battersea Beer festival
www.swlcamra.org.uk
Bishop Auckland beer festival
www.clevelandcamra.org.uk
Bradford beer festival
www.bradfordcamra.co.uk
Chesterfield beer festival
www.chesterfieldbeerfestival.org.uk
Dorchester beer festival
www.wessexcamra.org.uk/beerfestivals
Dover winter festival
www.camra-dds.org.uk
Fleetwood beer festival
www.blackpoolcamra.org.uk
Gosport beer festival
www.edgworth-real-ale-festival.co.uk
Hucknall beer festival
www.mansfieldcamra.org.uk
Liverpool beer festival
www.merseycamra.org.uk
Twickenham beer festival
www.rhcamra.org.uk
Rotherham beer festival
www.rotherhamcamra.co.uk
Salisbury beer festival
www.wiltshiretouristguide.com

Stockton-on-Tees beer festival
www.clevelandcamra.org.uk
Tewkesbury beer festival
www.tewkesburycamra.org.uk
Wear Valley beer festival
www.darlocamra.org.uk

MARCH
Bristol beer festival
www.camrabristol.org.uk
Darlington spring festival
www.darlocamra.org.uk
Ely beer festival
www.elycamra.org.uk
Hitchin beer festival
www.camranorthherts.org.uk
Leeds beer festival
www.leedsbeerfestival.co.uk
Leicester beer festival
www.leicestercamra.org.uk
London Drinker festival
www.camranorthlondon.org.uk
Mansfield beer festival
www.mansfieldcamra.org.uk
Oldham beer festival
www.robcamra.org.uk
Sussex/Brighton beer festival
www.visitbrighton.com
Thanet Easter Beer Festival
(Margate)
www.easterbeerfestival.org.uk
Wigan beer festival
www.wigancamra.org.uk
Winslow Beer Festival
www.winslowlions.org.uk/beerfestival
York beer festival
www.yorkcamra.free-online.co.uk

APRIL
Bury St Edmunds beer festival
www.cam.net.uk
Chippenham beer festival
www.nwwiltscamra.org.uk
Coventry
www.leicestercamra.org.uk
Dunstable
www.huntscamra.org.uk/festival
Farnham
www.camrasurrey.org.uk
Maldon beer festival
www.camra.org.uk/event
Mansfield beer festival
www.mansfieldcamra.org.uk
Newcastle upon Tyne beer festival
www.cannybevvy.co.uk
Oldham beer festival
www.robcamra.org.uk
Paisley beer festival
www.paisleybeerfestival.org.uk
Walsall beer festival
www.birminghamcamra.org.uk/Walsall
Wear Valley beer festival
www.darlocamra.org.uk

MAY
Banbury beer festival
www.northoxfordshirecamra.org.uk
Chester beer festival
www.chestercamra.co.uk
Ealing beer festival
www.ealingbeerfestival.org.uk
Macclesfield beer festival
www.maccbeerfestival.ndo.co.uk
Newark beer festival
www.newarkcamra.org.uk
Northampton beer festival
www.northantscamra.org.uk
Reading beer festival
www.readingbeerfestival.org.uk

Rugby beer festival
www.rugbycamra.org.uk
St Ives, Cornwall beer festival
www.staustellbrewery.co.uk
Stockport beer festival
www.ssmcamra.org.uk
Stourbridge beer festival
www.stourbridge-camra.co.uk
Thurrock beer festival
www.essex-camra.org.uk
Wolverhampton beer festival
www.wolverhamptoncamra.org.uk
Yapton beer festival
www.westernsussexcamra.org.uk

JUNE
Ashfield beer festival
www.mansfieldcamra.org.uk
Devizes festival
www.visitcotswoldsandsevernvale.gov.uk
Catford beer festival
www.selcamra.org.uk
Hereford beer festival
www.herefordcamra.freeuk.com
Kingston (Surrey) beer festival
www.camrasurrey.org.uk/kingston
Northampton beer festival
www.northantscamra.org.uk
North Devon beer festival
www.totaltravel.co.uk/travel/West-Country/north-devon/directory/events
Scottish Traditional Beer Festival, Edinburgh
www.edinburghcamra.org.uk/inkfestival.com
Southampton beer festival
www.shantscamra.org.uk
South Downs (Sussex) beer festival
www.brightoncamra.org.uk

Woodchurch, near Ashford, Kent beer festival
www.camra-afrm.org.uk

JULY
Ardingly beer festival
www.camrasurrey.org.uk
Boston beer festival
www.camra.org.uk
Boxmoor (Hemel Hempstead) beer festival
www.midchilternscamra.org.uk
Bromsgrove beer festival
www.camra.co.uk
Canterbury beer festival
www.kentbeerfestival.co.uk
Chelmsford summer festival
www.chelmsfordcamra.org.uk
Cotswolds beer festival
www.visitcotswoldsandsevernvale.gov.uk
Ealing beer festival
www.ealingbeerfestival.org.uk
Hereford beer festival
www.herefordcamra.freeuk.com
Plymouth beer festival
www.plymouthcamra.co.uk
Hereford beer festival
www.herefordcamra.freeuk.com
Louth beer festival
www.mansfieldcamra.org.uk
Much Wenlock beer festival
www.muchwenlockguide.info

AUGUST
Great British Beer Festival, London, Earls Court
www.camra.co.uk
Clacton beer festival
www.clactonbeerfestival.org.uk

Heart of Warwickshire beer
festival
www.camrahow.org.uk
Harbury beer festival
www.camrahow.org.uk
Moorgreen beer festival
www.moorgreenshow.co.uk
Peterborough beer festival
www.beer-fest.org.uk
Mumbles, Swansea beer festival
www.mumblesbeerfestival.com
Worcester beer festival
www.worcesterbeerfest.org.uk

SEPTEMBER
Ayrshire beer festival
www.ayrshirebeerfestival.co.uk
Birmingham beer festival
www.birminghamcamra.org.uk
Burton-on-Trent beer festival
www.burtoncamra.org.uk
Chappel (Essex) beer festival
www.camra.org.uk
Darlington beer festival
www.darlocamra.org.uk
Hull beer festival
www.hullcamra.org.uk
Ipswich beer festival
www.ipswichcamra.com
Jersey beer festival
www.camrajersey.org.je
Keighley beer festival
www.keighleyandcravencamra.org.uk
Letchworth beer festival
www.camranorthherts.org.uk
Maidstone beer festival
www.visitkent.co.uk
Melton Mowbray beer festival
www.camra.org.uk/event
Nantwich beer festival
www.outinncheshire.co.uk

Norths Notts beer festival
www.camrahantsnorth.org.uk
Northwich beer festival
www.northwichbeerfestival.co.uk
Portsmouth beer festival
www.pompeybeerfestival.co.uk
St Albans beer festival
www.hertsale.org.uk/beerfest
St Ives, Cambs beer festival
www.cambridge-camra.org.uk
Scunthorpe beer festival
www.northlincs.gov.uk
Sheffield beer festival
www.sheffieldcamra.co.uk
Shrewsbury beer festival
www.shrewsburycamra.org.uk
Somerset beer festival
www.newtbeerfest.com
Southport beer festival
www.southportcamra.org.uk
South Devon beer festival
www.southdevoncamra.com
Tamworth beer festival
www.last-orders-camra.org.uk
Troon beer festival
www.troonfest.org.uk
Ulverston beer festival
www.furnesscamra.co.uk

OCTOBER
Bath beer festival
www.bathandborderscamra.org.uk
Bedford beer festival
www.northbedscamra.org.uk
Birkenhead/Wirral beer festival
www.camrawirral.org.uk
Boston beer festival
www.camra.org.uk
Bridgenorth/SVR beer festival
www.mansfieldcamra.org.uk

Carmarthen beer festival
www.thebestof.co.uk/carmarthen
Croydon beer festival
www.croydoncamra.org.uk
Dunfermline beer festival
www.thebestof.co.uk/fife
Eastbourne beer festival
www.eastbournebeerfestival.co.uk
Falmouth beer festival
www.siba.co.uk/calendar
Gravesend beer festival
www.gravesend-camra-beer-
festival.org.uk
Harlow beer festival
www.camranorthlondon.org.uk
Huddersfield beer festival
www.camra.org.uk
Norwich beer festival
www.norwichcamra.org.uk
Nottingham beer festival
www.nottinghamcamra.org
Overton beer festival
www.overtonbeerfestival.org.uk
Oxford beer festival
oxfordcamra.org.uk
Poole beer festival
www.eastdorsetcamra.org
Redhill beer festival
camrasurrey.org.uk/redhill
Solihull beer festival
www.solihullcamra.org.uk
Stalybridge beer festival
www.foodanddrinkfestival.com
Stoke-on-Trent beer festival
www.camrapotteries.co.uk
Swindon beer festival
www.swindoncamra.org.uk
Twickenham beer festival
www.rhcamra.org.uk
Wakefield beer festival
www.camra.co.uk

Westmorland/Kendall beer festival
www.camrawestmorland.org
Worthing beer festival
www.aaa-camra.org.uk

NOVEMBER
Aberdeen beer festival
aberdeencamra.co.uk
Belfast beer festival
www.camrani.org.uk
Dudley winter festival
www.dudleycamra.org.uk
Eastleigh (Hants) beer festival
www.shantscamra.org.uk
Erewash beer fetival
www.erewash-camra.org
Great Welsh Beer & Cider Festival
www.gwbcf.cardiffcamra.co.uk
Hull beer festival
www.hullcamra.org.uk
Luton beer festival
www.sbedscamra.org.uk
Medway beer festival
medwaybeerfestival.com
Rochford beer festival
www.camra.org.uk
Watford beer festival
www.watfordcamra.org.uk
Wirral beer festival
www.camrawirral.org.uk
Woking beer festival
www.wokingbeerfestival.co.uk

DECEMBER
Cockermouth beer festival
www.cockermouthbeerfestival.co.uk
Harwich beer festival
www.harwich.net/beerfest

All info correct at time of going to press.

Pub quiz

Answers

1. Melchester   2. For winning the US Masters and Tour de France   3. Juniper
4. Susan   5. Jules Rimet Trophy   6. Work   7. Bitter   8. False, they're knots
9. 35-1   10. £50   11. In a hot dog roll   12. Superman (by 11 months)
13. Weightlifting   14. Sherry   15. Robert Louis Stevenson   16. Garibaldi
17. Beer (Shlitz)   18. Three years   19. 1930s   20. William Pitt the Younger
21. Cocoa beans   22. 432   23. Bordeaux   24. Mexico   25. Avocados
26. Fruit or seeds   27. Pears   28. Hops   29. Dill   30. Bobby Charlton
31. Rover's Return   32. Woolpack   33. Teenage Kicks   34. Black Velvet
35. Tetleys   36. Castlemaine   37. Getting the beers in   38. Town Hall
39. Duff   40. Nine gallons   41. 20fl oz   42. Pilchard   43. Maths
44. Crushed insects   45. Watford   46. Delia Smith   47. France
48. Peru and Bolivia   49. 1F, 2J, 3C, 4H, 5I, 6D, 7A, 8G, 9B, 10E

MORRISSEY MAXIM

Better to have a safety wank before a first date than a couple of Dutch courage drinks. In other words, don't go out with a loaded gun.

Index

Morrissey and Foxy's thanks go to ...

... the hundreds of people we've shared top times with over the years in hostelries across the globe. Except due to the quality and quantity of imbibing, our memories for the names and faces are mostly too vague to fully recall, but thanks all the same – you (may) remember who you are.

As far as current projects and good times go, we would like to thank our wonderful friends at HarperCollins such as Jenny Heller, Lesley Robb, Richard Marston and Martin Toseland for their support and enthusiasm for all things beer. Similarly, the wonderful folk at Fresh 1, Talkback Thames, and Ch4 who have been similarly enthused – we salute you.

We'd also like to take this opportunity to thank our fabulous team at Ye Olde Punch Bowl in Marton cum Grafton for their hard-work, dedication and smiling through the hard times: Adam Gray, Gordon Gellatly, Helen Cawkwell and the rest of Ye Olde crew – top job guys.

Thanks to Adam Lugge of the Noble in Crouch Hill for the use of the bar and the delicious pub grub he served up.

As far as our personal brewing journey goes, it's a case of: the beers are on us for the wonderful Roosters family: Sean, Sam and Alison for vision and inspiration in the art of beer making. A massive 'lets have a night out' to the Cropton boys – Phil, Paul and Richard for being true brewing heroes who have become our great friends during this bleary journey.

Finally, special thanks love and respect to Chris and Julie Hamilton, Tim and Nicky Ashton, Emma Killick and of course, the irrepressible Tiggy. And a huge big-up to all our friends and customers, without whose support, we'd still be staring at the dregs at the bottom of someone else's beer. Cheers!

First published in 2008 by Collins, an imprint of HarperCollins*Publishers*,
77–85 Fulham Palace Road, Hammersmith, London w6 8jb

www.collins.co.uk

Collins is a registered trademark of HarperCollins*Publishers* Ltd

Text©HarperCollins
Cover photography©Adam Lawrence
Design and layout©HarperCollins*Publishers* Ltd

A catalogue record for this book is available from the British Library.

Editorial Director: Jenny Heller
Editor: Lesley Robb
Research: Trevor Kite
Designer: Richard '*mash tun*' Marston
Photography: Getty Images, Shutterstock, Richard Marston
Cover design: Anna Martin
Cover photographer: Adam Lawrence
Senior Production Controller: Chris Gurney

ISBN 978-0-00-728468-9

Printed and bound by Rotolito, Italy